Student Success

Essay Writing

Skills

Expository Essay Techniques

Ashan R. Hampton

Onyx Publishing
Arkansas

Published by Onyx Online Education & Training, Little Rock, Arkansas.
Imprint: Lulu.com.

For bulk orders and book discounts, see the website at www.arhampton.com/onyxbooks.

Cover Design: Ashan R. Hampton

Cover Photo: © *Can Stock Photo/ deandrobot*

Websites: www.arhampton.com
www.onyxonlineedu.com

Library of Congress Control Number: 2021900695
ISBN: 978-1-716-23704-1

Printed in the United States of America.

First Edition.

Cataloging-in-Publication Data is on file with the Library of Congress.

10 9 8 7 6 5 4 3 2 1

Student Success

Online Classes

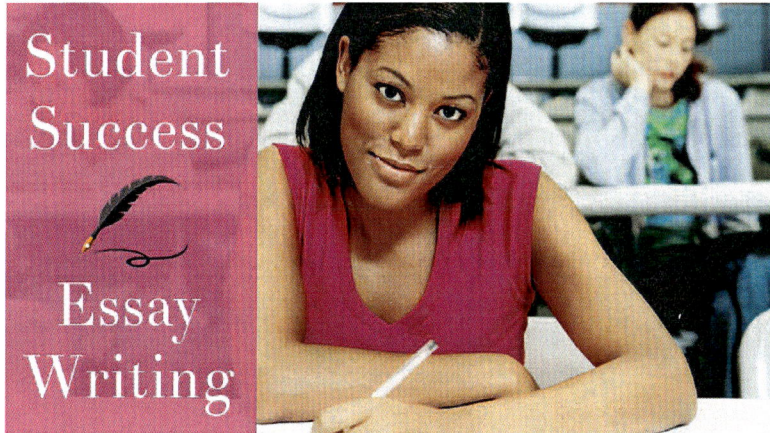

Student Success Grammar

Student Success Writing Skills

Student Success Essay Writing

Graduate Research Writing Skills

www.arhampton.com/classes
www.arhampton.com/students

About the Author

Ashan R. Hampton has worked as an English instructor in higher education for over 20 years, most notably at Morehouse College in Atlanta, Georgia. She is also a proud graduate of the *Donaghey Scholars Program* at the University of Arkansas at Little Rock under the direction of Dr. C. Earl Ramsey, Emeritus.

Ashan's original research, *History of the Arkansas State Hospital 1859-1930*, was published in the *Pulaski County Historical Review* (1995) and continues to be cited by history scholars today. Her articles on notable African American Arkansans also appear in the *Encyclopedia of Arkansas History and Culture*.

With her doctoral studies on hold, Ashan has found success in online education. She produces and teaches her own writing and grammar courses for global audiences through her company, *Onyx Online Education & Training*. She has also worked full-time as a technical writer, digital media coordinator, web designer and legal editor.

Visit her website: **www.arhampton.com**.

Contents

Introduction

As a young teacher and adjunct English instructor, I was often tasked with instructing Composition I courses. These classes teach about the writing process and different expository writing techniques. I would try to make the courses more robust by including grammar boosters, since good writing starts with good grammar. After spending years of teaching lower-level writing courses, I finally decided to stop. However, as I looked over all of the slides, handouts, and video assets I had developed, it occurred to me that other teachers could also benefit from my treasure trove of instructional resources.

This book, *"Student Success Essay Writing Skills,"* is an extension of those resources. With the new demands of virtual learning, high school and college students alike still need good, solid instruction on how to write essays on different topics from a variety of perspectives. Additionally, teachers and homeschool parents need trustworthy materials to refer to when tutoring and assisting students with their assignments. So, this book covers all of the expository essays that are usually assigned in a college composition class, which also supports college readiness standards for graduating high school seniors and adult education (GED) students.

After introducing readers to the writing process and how to write complex paragraphs, the chapters cover the most common essay types taught to students in preparation for standardized testing and the rigor of writing college level assignments and research papers. These old standards include **narration, description, illustration, definition, process, comparison/contrast, cause/effect, classification, and argument essays**.

Yes, you're welcome! It is not always easy to find genuinely well-crafted information on this subject from a highly qualified English instructor, so this book is extremely valuable to everyone who needs to improve their writing skills and progress well in their studies. This book closes with two exciting sections on expanding essays with details and how to draft clear and concise writing. If you favor audio/visual instruction, you might want to consider enrolling in the **online course** of the same title that complements this book. You can find details and a full curriculum list at www.arhampton.com/classes.

Chapter One
The Writing Process

Photo by Avel Truklanov from Unsplash.

What is the Writing Process?

Have you ever experienced writer's block? Perhaps you have a report or an essay due, but you just do not know where to start. Well, the steps of the writing process take you from a blank page to a written document. Instead of just staring at a computer screen and waiting for inspiration, sometimes you have to start small by jotting down words, phrases and finally, complete sentences. The six major steps of the writing process actually include several micro-activities that ease you into writing a full-length document. Although some resources cite more than six steps, the following are generally agreed upon in most reference books:

Steps of the Writing Process:

1. Exploring Ideas
2. Prewriting
3. Organizing
4. Writing
5. Revising
6. Producing (Final Copy)

Step One: Exploring Ideas

The first step in the writing process is to get clear about your subject matter. **What are you writing about?** What topic or ideas do you need to inform someone about? For example, if you need to write a job aid handout on how to access a school's new grading software system, then what is your subject? **The new grading software system.**

:: Consider the Subject ::

Now that you know the subject matter of the job aid handout, everything you write will focus on the new grading software system and nothing else. You should not mention another similar system or the old system, because those are irrelevant to the reader. Only include information that will help teachers learn to use the new grading software system. This micro-activity is called *considering your subject.*

:: Consider the Purpose ::

Why are you talking about this subject matter? In keeping with our example above, why are you writing about the new grading software system? Is your purpose simply to inform employees about this new system or to get them to access the system within a certain number of days?

Perhaps midterm grade reports will not be mailed, but will only be available in the new system. So, parents must access the system to download and print their children's report cards. In this scenario, **the purpose is to get parents to access the new grading software system.**

In general, **the purpose of your writing** will fall into one of three categories:

1. to inform
2. to persuade
3. to entertain

:: Consider the Audience ::

Who are you writing for? The audience consists of the people who will read your writing. Your audience will vary depending on the situation and the purpose of your writing. For example, who will more than likely read the job aid on accessing the new grading software system?

- Teachers
- School Employees
- Parents

To further understand how your subject, purpose and audience connect, you might need to jot down an **audience analysis**. Why? Because before you begin to write, you must get clear on your subject, audience, and purpose.

1.	**Subject**	the new grading software system
2.	**Audience**	teachers, school employees, parents
3.	**Purpose**	to inform

At times, you might need to adjust your writing for your audience. For example, what if you need to inform internal employees and the general public of the new electronic paystub system? In this situation, the content, format and purpose of your writing will change depending on your audience.

Subject: the new electronic paystub system	**Subject:** the new grading software system
Audience: teachers/employees	**Audience:** parents
Purpose: to inform	**Purpose:** to inform
Format: a job aid handout	**Format:** a printed letter
Content: • Discuss the new system • Replacing old system • How to access the new system	**Content:** • Discuss the new system • Benefits of new system • How to access the new system

Step Two: Prewriting

Prewriting consists of strategies that help you generate ideas and main points of support for your topic. Prewriting is also commonly referred to as brainstorming where you jot down or list ideas in simple words or short phrases. The goal is to stir your thinking about the subject and inspire you to get your ideas down on paper before attempting to compose a full document.

:: Freewriting ::

Free writing is when you allow yourself a specified amount of time to write anything that comes to mind about your topic with no regard to organization, grammar, or editing. For example, imagine that you are writing a speech on the importance of community colleges. Set a timer for 10 minutes and write anything that comes to mind about the benefits of community college to high school graduates. While freewriting, your pen never stops or leaves the page.

:: Questioning ::

The **questioning** technique involves providing answers to ***The Five Ws and One H***, also referred to as ***The Six Ws***. In the world of journalism, these are also called **reporter's questions**, because every story must answer these basic six elements of storytelling.

The Five Ws and One H:
- Who?
- What?
- When?
- Why?
- Where?
- How?

Regardless of what you are writing, these questions should guide your prewriting or brainstorming sessions as an individual or as a team. This is particularly true in the world of project management where group projects can get muddled and confusing very quickly. Before undertaking complex tasks or writing assignments, step back and answer these six questions before moving ahead. Understanding the fundamental direction of your subject matter allows your writing to flow a lot easier.

:: Journaling ::

Journaling involves using a notebook to write raw, private thoughts about your subject. This technique usually applies to personal, narrative, persuasive or fiction writing. However, in the business world, journaling can help you compose a resignation or a complaint letter, or any type of writing that might trigger an emotional response that needs to be delivered in a focused, professional manner.

:: Clustering ::

Clustering involves drawing graphical circles labeled with words or phrases that present your ideas. The main idea of your subject matter is centered in the middle circle. Each related idea that branches from it will become the main points in the body of your writing project. For example, if you were writing a five-paragraph essay, the middle would name your subject and the branched ideas would illustrate the three main points of your essay. Since all writing must contain a beginning, middle and end, the clustering technique can be applied to any form of business writing, not just academic essays.

Example of Clustering:

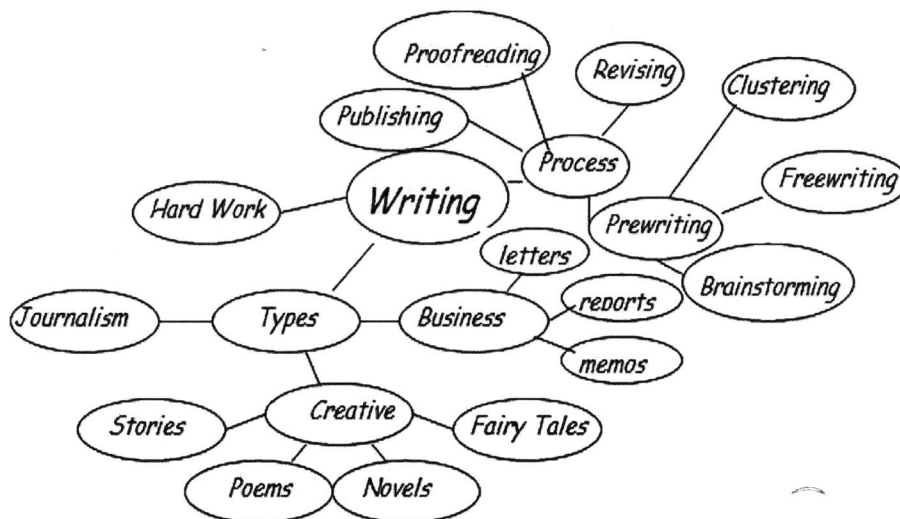

Step Three: Organizing

As mentioned earlier, every piece of writing must include a beginning, middle and end—an introduction, a body, and a conclusion. This is the fundamental organizing structure for any writing project. The only thing that changes within this structure is the subject, style, complexity and length of the content, whether you are writing a change of teacher request to a school principal or a grant proposal for a new literacy program.

:: Project Organizing Structure ::

Every writing project contains an:

- Introduction
- Body
- Conclusion

Now that you have a sense of your subject, audience, purpose, format and content, it is time to start thinking about what information will come first, next and last. What background information will you put in the introduction? What are the three main points of your writing? What kinds of information will you include to illustrate or support those points in the body of your writing? How will you conclude? All of these considerations comprise the process of organizing your document.

In a nutshell, you are selecting the details to include in the final version of your document, which requires some degree of outlining. At this point, you must create an informal or formal outline to properly arrange your ideas.

:: Outlining ::

An **informal outline** can include main headings and bullet points, which are handwritten or typed on one page. A **formal outline** is more suited for long, complex documents, because it includes main points, subpoints, roman numerals and alphabetical lists. The goal of any outline is to focus your ideas in a clear, logical fashion, which makes the actual writing process easier and faster.

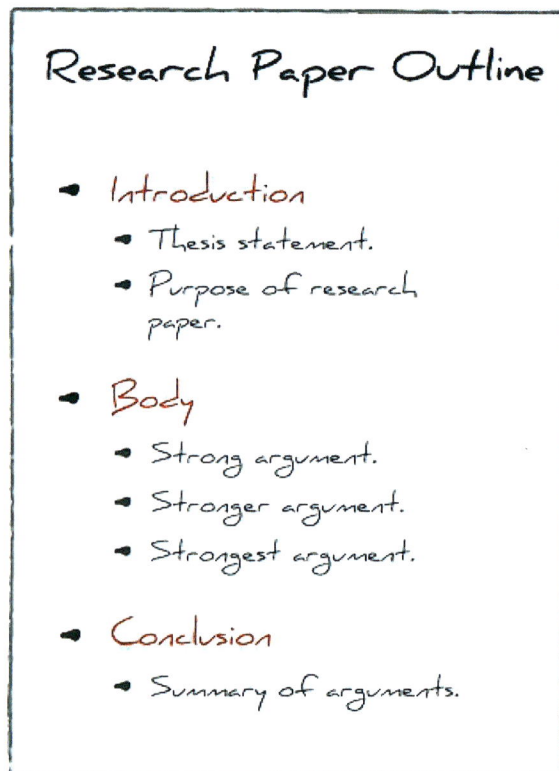

Research Paper Outline

- Introduction
  - Thesis statement.
  - Purpose of research paper.

- Body
  - Strong argument.
  - Stronger argument.
  - Strongest argument.

- Conclusion
  - Summary of arguments.

Step Four: Writing the First Draft

After all of the planning and organizing, now you must write! Using the notes from your outline, formulate your ideas into full sentences and paragraphs. Your writing does not need to be perfect at this point. Use your outline to fill in the content of your document. For some people, writing long-hand is a good way to start, because it keeps them from getting distracted by computer keyboards or alerts popping up on a screen. However, some people prefer to type out their first draft. Choose the writing technique that works best for you.

Step Five: Revising the Draft

In this stage, you want your writing to be as clear and error-free as possible. At this point in the writing process, you are trying to finalize the draft by adding, deleting or rearranging your content. You are putting all of your details in order and editing for clarity. If you are collaborating on a paper, now is the time to incorporate comments and suggestions from your team. The goal of revising the draft is to get the document as clean as possible before producing the final copy.

:: Tips for Revising Your Draft ::

One likely reason for these lackluster long-term results is that a low-carbohydrate diet—like any restrictive diet—is difficult to adhere to for any extended period. ~~Most people enjoy foods that are high in carbohydrates, and no one wants to be the person who always turns down that slice of pizza or birthday cake.~~ In commenting on the Gardner study, experts at the Harvard School of Public Health (2010) noted that women in all four diet groups had difficulty following the plan. Because it is hard for dieters to stick to a low-carbohydrate eating plan, the initial success of these diets is short-lived (Heinz, 2009). Medical professionals caution that low-carbohydrate diets are difficult for many people to follow consistently and that, to maintain a healthy weight, dieters should try to develop nutrition and exercise habits they can incorporate in their lives in the long term (Mayo Clinic, 2008). Registered dietician Dana Kwon (2010) comments, "For some people, [low-carbohydrate diets] are great, but for most, any sensible eating and exercise plan would work just as well" (Kwon, 2010).

- Read the first draft.

- Cut parts that do not fit your subject, audience or purpose.

- Add information, if necessary.

- Rearrange sentences in the paragraph.

- Rearrange paragraphs to flow in a logical order.

- Rewrite sentences for clarity.

- Read your document out loud. This will help you hear mistakes that your natural eyes might miss.

Step Six: Producing the Final Copy

Depending on the sophistication of your essay assignment, getting to this final stage could take hours, days, months or years. For example, a research paper could take two weeks or an effective master's thesis could take six months to a year to complete. In either case, the goal is to get the final document ready for print and distribution.

1. Print out a typed draft of your paper. This should be your second time printing and reading the document.

2. Edit your document. Carefully read and examine the document for errors.

3. Use a red pen to help you see errors on the printed draft.

4. Correct all errors including typos, misspelled words, grammar, punctuation, incomplete sentences, omitted words, and other mistakes.

5. After making all edits to your writing, print another copy of the paper. This should be your third printed copy.

6. Proofread your paper. Remember, proofreading is not the same as editing. To learn more about the differences, get your copy of the book, *Proofreading Power: Skills & Drills* from **www.arhampton.com**.

7. Get another person to check your writing for errors.

8. If a second reader finds more errors, fix them and print your document for a fourth review.

9. Give yourself enough time to take a break and read the document again with fresh eyes.

10. Print and read the paper again—for the fifth and final time—to correct all errors before submitting the final copy.

Summary: The Writing Process

When you think about the consequences of leaving mistakes in your written document, you will find that printing your paper five times for editing and proofreading is not excessive at all. You must continue to edit and proofread, until every error has been corrected. Every step in the writing process is necessary. Attempting to skip steps will cost you a lot of time, money and frustration. Although it might seem daunting, following the steps in order will allow you to write faster and more efficiently.

In Summary:

- Consider the subject.

- Consider the purpose.

- Consider the audience.

- Prewrite and organize your ideas.

- Write.

- Revise, edit, and proofread.

Good Writing Starts with Good Grammar!

Student Success Grammar Skills

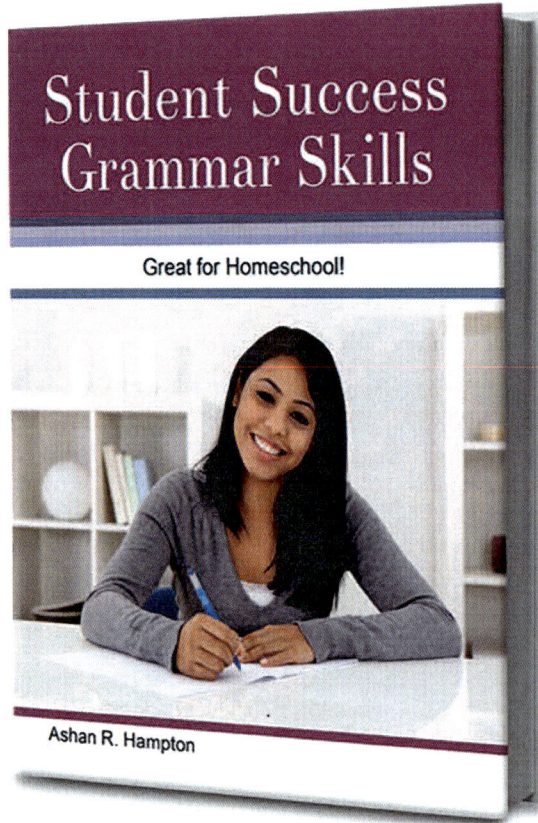

124 pages
ISBN: 978-0-359-60763-1

Before students can write successful classroom assignments, they must know grammar. "Student Success Grammar Skills," makes it easy for middle school, high school, college students and adult learners to improve their language and writing abilities. In this book, students learn to effectively put words and phrases together before tackling essays, research papers, and other longer, written documents.

****

Order your copies today!

www.arhampton.com/books

Writing Process Exercise

Directions: Put the steps of the writing process in order by numbering them 1 through 4.

_____ Proofreading

_____ Revising

_____ Prewriting

_____ Writing the first draft

Directions: Read the paragraph and then answer the questions that follow by circling the letter of the correct response.

Coffee drinkers should seriously consider switching to tea. According to the latest research, the ingredients in tea may help people stay slim. When Taiwanese researchers studied 1,000 people, they found that the people who drank two cups of any kind of tea every week for ten years had 20 percent less body fat than people who didn't drink tea. But there's an even better reason to switch. As it turns out, tea lowers the risk of serious disease, such as some cancers, heart attack, and stroke. In 2003, scientists found out that after just three weeks of drinking five cups of black tea per day, 15 people cut their cholesterol by seven percent and their bad LDL cholesterol by 11 percent. Australian researchers studying 218 women found that tea reduced blood pressure; in fact, the more tea a person drank, the more blood pressure dropped. Coffee does not offer any of these health benefits, so tea is clearly the better beverage choice.

1. **This paragraph was written for an audience of**
    a. tea drinkers.
    b. coffee drinkers.
    c. researchers.

2. **The subject of this paragraph is**
    a. the benefits of drinking tea.
    b. healthy beverages.
    c. coffee drinkers.

3. **The purpose of this paragraph is to**
    a. explain the differences between coffee and tea.
    b. persuade coffee drinkers to drink tea instead.
    c. convince people to drink healthy beverages.

Answers: Writing Process Exercise

4   Proofreading

3   Revising

1   Prewriting

2   Writing the first draft

1. **This paragraph was written for an audience of**
    a. tea drinkers.
    b. coffee drinkers.
    c. researchers.

2. **The subject of this paragraph is**
    a. the benefits of drinking tea.
    b. healthy beverages.
    c. coffee drinkers.

3. **The purpose of this paragraph is to**
    a. explain the differences between coffee and tea.
    b. persuade coffee drinkers to drink tea instead.
    c. convince people to drink healthy beverages.

Chapter Two
How to Write Paragraphs

Photo by Pexels.

What is a Paragraph?

A **paragraph** is a group of related sentences that develop one main idea. This main idea is expressed in the **topic sentence**, which is the first sentence in a paragraph. All of the lines that give details about the main topic are called **supporting sentences**. Short paragraphs are about 3-5 sentences long, while complex paragraphs contain at least 5-7 sentences, but no more than 10 sentences. In general, paragraphs are groups of words that are used to create an essay, report, or any other longer piece of writing.

What is a Topic Sentence?

The topic **sentence** is usually the very first sentence of the paragraph. The topic sentence suggests what the rest of the paragraph will talk about. Topic sentences are general enough to introduce the main idea of a paragraph without giving specific details.

What are Supporting Sentences?

- **Supporting sentences** follow the topic sentence.

- **Supporting sentences** give more details and specific information about the main topic of the paragraph.

- As a student writer, you must create your own supporting sentences without relying on other authors or outside research. However, you can summarize or paraphrase outside research articles by expressing the author's main ideas in your own words.

- The kind of supporting sentences you create depends on the type of essay you are writing.

Effective Paragraph Example

Playing video games may give doctors an advantage in the operating room, helping them save lives. A 2004 research study at New York's Beth Israel Medical Center tested thirty-three doctors on video game tasks that measured their motor skills, reaction time, and hand-eye coordination. These are the same skills that are essential to performing laparoscopic surgery, which involves using a joystick to maneuver a tiny video camera inserted into a patient's body. Researchers found that doctors who used to play video games for more than three hours a week were 37 percent less likely than non-gamers to make mistakes. They also finished procedures 27 percent faster than non-gamers.

Topic Sentence: Playing video games may give doctors an advantage in the operating room, helping them save lives.

Supporting Sentences: All of the underlined sentences in the above paragraph are called supporting sentences, because they give more details about the main topic sentence. Sometimes supporting sentences include research facts, quotes, or statistics from outside sources.

Knowledge Check

1. Where does the **topic sentence** appear in a paragraph?

2. What information do supporting sentences give?

3. What details count as outside research in the above paragraph?

Ineffective Paragraph Example

There have been several problems with following our safety guidelines over the last month. It is Mary's birthday tomorrow, so please stop by the front desk to donate toward her celebration lunch. Progress reports are due in Mr. Blandin's office by noon today. Whenever I see a customer at the warehouse, I try to be friendly and helpful.

- **What is wrong with this short paragraph?** It does not focus on one main idea.
- According to the topic sentence, the paragraph should discuss several problems with safety guidelines.
- However, all of the supporting sentences talk about something different that does not relate to the topic sentence. For example, Mary's birthday, progress reports, and customer service.
- Since none of the sentences give details about problems with safety guidelines, this is an ineffective paragraph, because the supporting sentences are not unified around one main idea.

What Do You Mean by Unified?

A paragraph should focus on one main idea, not several. When one paragraph contains several ideas, it is considered disjointed, unsupported or not unified. Differing ideas should be broken up into separate paragraphs with their own topic sentences.

Example of a Disjointed (Unsupported) Paragraph:

My brother got his GED last year, and now he has a good job. I need a good job too. I left high school when I was a freshman and never went back. If I get a GED my kids will look up to me. If I get a better job, I will make more money. I need money to move to a bigger apartment because my kids are getting older and need more room.

What is wrong with the above paragraph?

This paragraph includes more than one main idea: good job, kids, more money. Therefore, it is not unified and does not qualify as a good paragraph.

Example of a Unified (Supported) Paragraph:

Getting a GED will make my life better by improving my career options. With a GED, I can get a better job. At my company, you need a GED or high school diploma to work as a customer service representative. If I get a job as a CSR, I can move out of the warehouse and make more money working in the call center. The increase in my salary will allow me to move into a bigger apartment or a townhouse. Since my kids are getting older, they need more room to finish their homework and entertain their friends. Right now, I can only afford a small two-bedroom apartment where my two children have to share a room. So, getting a GED will give me better career choices and help make a better life for me and my children.

Why is this paragraph better?

This paragraph focuses on one main idea of improving career options. All of the supporting sentences center around how this person can advance to a better career by getting a GED. Every sentence describes in detail why this is important to receiving better career choices. Therefore, this is considered a good unified paragraph.

Key Points for Writing Good Paragraphs

- Paragraphs must begin with a good topic sentence.

- Placing the topic sentence at the beginning of the paragraph reduces confusion for the reader and keeps the paragraph unified around one main idea.

- Ideas in a paragraph should flow logically from sentence to sentence.

- The sentences should be arranged in a logical order: general to specific, chronological (time order); top to bottom (spatial order), etc.

- The last sentence in the paragraph should give a sense of conclusion by reiterating the main idea in the topic sentence without repeating the topic sentence.

- Often, the last sentence will be written as a transition into the next body paragraph of an essay.

- Remember, a topic sentence and a thesis are two different things. A topic sentence is the first line of a paragraph, whereas a thesis is usually the last sentence of the introductory paragraph in an essay.

How Do You Write a Paragraph?

1. First, make sure your idea for a paragraph fits the topic or prompt.
2. Second, brainstorm ideas for a paragraph by making a list.
3. Next, decide which ideas to drop or keep.
4. Arrange the phrases from the list into groups of similar ideas.
5. Write the phrases from the list into full sentences.
6. Write the first draft of the paragraph.
7. Add more details or subtract irrelevant details to make the paragraph unified.
8. Edit and revise as necessary.
9. Write and proofread the final draft.

Now, let's put these nine steps for writing a paragraph into action.

Topic/Prompt: Describe a memorable job or office space.

Your idea: Describe your manager's messy office space.

1. Brainstorm details & supporting sentences for paragraph:

- His office is full of crumpled paper, sticky notes all over the cubicle walls, candy wrappers on the desk; overflowing waste basket
- His favorite candy is *Hershey's Kisses*
- He often arrives late to meetings
- When the workers complained of a foul smell, maintenance found a rotten peach in the bottom of his desk drawer
- His sister who works on the ninth floor is just as messy
- Stacks of old newspapers sit on chair seats
- He is one messy person
- Papers for meetings are often stained with coffee or chocolate
- He jots meeting information on sticky notes that he forgets about
- Because of his messiness, supervisors and staff do not like working with him

2. Drop or Keep: Cross Out the Irrelevant Details

- His office is full of crumpled paper, sticky notes all over the cubicle walls, candy wrappers on the desk; overflowing waste basket
- ~~His favorite candy is *Hershey's Kisses*~~
- He often arrives late to meetings
- When the workers complained of a foul smell, maintenance found a rotten peach in the bottom of his desk drawer
- ~~His sister who works on the ninth floor is just as messy~~
- Stacks of old newspapers sit on chair seats
- ~~He is one messy person~~
- Papers for meetings are often stained with coffee or chocolate
- He jots meeting information on sticky notes that he forgets about
- Because of his messiness, supervisors and staff do not like working with him

---

3. Group the ideas from the list above into related sections.

APPEARANCE OF OFFICE

- His office is full of crumpled paper, sticky notes all over the cubicle walls, candy wrappers on the desk; overflowing waste basket
- Stacks of old newspapers sit on chair seats
- Foul smell, rotten peach in the bottom desk drawer

MEETINGS/ PERFORMANCE

- He often arrives late to meetings
- Papers for meetings are often stained with coffee or chocolate
- He jots meeting information on sticky notes that he forgets about
- Because of his messiness, supervisors and staff do not like working with him

4. Putting it all together:

First Draft

One of the managers at my job has the messiest office space on the entire floor. His office is full of crumpled paper, sticky notes all over the cubicle walls, candy wrappers on the desk, overflowing waste basket. Stacks of old newspapers sit on chair seats. When the workers complained of a foul smell, maintenance found a rotten peach in the bottom of his desk drawer. He jots meeting information on sticky notes that he forgets about. He often arrives late to meetings. Papers for meetings are often stained with coffee or chocolate. Because of his messiness, supervisors and staff do not like working with him.

Edit & Revise First Draft

One of the managers at my job has the messiest office space on the entire floor. ~~His~~Mr. Bob's office is full of crumpled paper, ~~sticky notes all over the cubicle walls, candy~~ Hershey's Kisses wrappers ~~on~~ all over the desk, an overflowing waste basket and multi-colored sticky notes all over the cubicle walls. Stacks of old newspapers sit on his only chair ~~seats~~for guests. When ~~the workers~~some employees complained of a foul smell, maintenance found a rotten, fuzzy peach in the bottom of his desk drawer. ~~He~~ Since Mr. Bob jots meeting information on sticky notes that he forgets about or cannot find, ~~.~~ ~~H~~he often arrives late to meetings. ~~His~~ ~~P~~papers for meetings are often stained with coffee or chocolate. Because of his ~~messiness~~untidiness and disorganization, supervisors and staff do not like working with him.

Final Draft

One of the managers at my job has the messiest office space on the entire floor. Mr. Bob's office is full of crumpled paper, Hershey's Kisses wrappers all over the desk, an overflowing waste basket and multi-colored sticky notes all over the cubicle walls. Stacks of old newspapers sit on his only chair for guests. When some employees complained of a foul smell, maintenance found a rotten, fuzzy peach in the bottom of his desk drawer. Since Mr. Bob jots meeting information on sticky notes that he forgets about or cannot find, he often arrives late to meetings. His papers for meetings are often stained with coffee or chocolate. Because of his untidiness and disorganization, supervisors and staff do not like working with him.

Paragraph Exercise

Directions: Choose the best topic sentence for each paragraph.

1. (1) Choose a quiet place in your home where you can work undisturbed. (2) Be sure to have plenty of pencils, pens, necessary books and paper within easy reach so that you do not have to waste time locating them. (3) Remember to ask family members to respect your needs to be alone and to concentrate. (4) Try to stick to studying one subject at a time, and allow plenty of time for each. (5) Finally, take breaks when you need to because studying is hard work.

Question: Which sentence below would be most effective at the beginning of the paragraph?

a. It is important to do well in school.

b. There are several things you can do to make study time more productive.

c. Children can be taught to work hard.

2. (1) First of all, the water that comes from your kitchen faucet may not be the best thing to drink. (2) The taste may be off because of chemicals present in your town's water source, and there is always the danger of harmful bacteria. (3) Second, bottled water can get very expensive. (4) The average cost for a half-gallon of bottled spring water is now more than $1.40 in many areas. (5) For these reasons, a pure oxygen water filtration system is the best water source for your family. (6) Call 1-800-555-1111 for more information.

Question: Which sentence below would be most effective at the beginning of the paragraph?

a. Your water may be too dangerous to drink.

b. Filtering your water at home is expensive and difficult.

c. A pure oxygen water filtration system is your family's best source of drinking water.

Answers: 1. b   2. c

Chapter Three
Complex Paragraphs

Photo by Cottonbro from Pexels.

What are Complex Paragraphs?

Complex Paragraphs include five (**5**) main parts:
1. **Topic** Sentence
2. **Support Sentence:** Lead-in
3. **Support Sentence:** Quoted Research
4. **Support Sentence:** Analysis
5. **Transition:** Concluding Sentence

As with any other paragraph, a **complex paragraph** must begin with a topic sentence to establish the main idea of the paragraph. All of the sentences after the topic sentence count as support.

For the analysis, never leave a quote from outside sources hanging. Always follow the quote with additional information that can lead to an enhanced understanding of how the idea in the quote relates to the main idea of your paper.

Transitional Phrases:

The last sentence of the paragraph should bridge into the next related idea that will be discussed in the next paragraph. Basically, the transition should set up or introduce the topic sentence of the next paragraph. In addition, the transitional sentence also serves as a concluding line to wrap up the paragraph before moving on to the next. Use **transitional words** and **phrases**, such as "in addition to," "next," or "unlike previous findings" to link sentences within a paragraph and to signify that another different idea is about to be discussed.

Types of Support

For complete definitions for the following types of information that can be used to create supporting sentences, read Chapter 14, "Expanding the Details" in this book.

Support for complex paragraphs can include:

- Anecdotes (brief stories)
- Quotes
- Statistics
- Authoritative sources
- Scientific research

Complex Paragraph Example

   The student population within higher education is rapidly changing. Gone are the days of the ruddy faced freshmen leaving their homes to experience their first taste of independence without parental intervention or control. In contrast, today's college students are more experienced, slightly older, socioeconomically disadvantaged and academically challenged. In a Chronicle of Higher Education article, Raising Graduation Rates Involves More Than Just Colleges, Espinosa (2010) describes these 21st century learners as, "those from growing racial and ethnic minority groups, those who are the first in their families to attend college, adult learners, and displaced workers." Unfortunately, these millennial students are also products of a broken, chaotic public education system that has rendered them unprepared for college level curriculums. However, the current economic crisis demands that workers possess higher skill levels and college degrees in order to become successful in today's fast- paced, global workplaces. As a result, more workers feel the pressure to enter college, and colleges feel the pressure to accommodate students who are academically unprepared for college life.

Complex Paragraph Breakdown

TOPIC SENTENCE: The student population within higher education is rapidly changing. Gone are the days of the ruddy faced freshmen leaving their homes to experience their first taste of independence without parental intervention or control. In contrast, today's college students are more experienced, slightly older, and academically challenged. **QUOTED RESEARCH SUPPORT:** In a Chronicle of Higher Education article, *Raising Graduation Rates Involves More Than Just Colleges*, Espinosa (2010) describes these 21st century learners as, "those from growing racial and ethnic minority groups, those who are the first in their families to attend college, adult learners, and displaced workers." **ANALYSIS:** Unfortunately, these millennial students are also products of a broken, chaotic public education system that has rendered them unprepared for college level curriculums. However, the current economic crisis demands that workers possess higher skill levels and college degrees in order to become successful in today's fast-paced, global workplaces. **TRANSITION:** As a result, more workers feel the pressure to enter college, and college institutions feel the pressure to accommodate students who are academically unprepared for college life.

Key Points for Complex Paragraphs

1. Include quotes from outside research sources.
2. Offer analysis.
3. Write transition statements.
4. These **three elements** are essential to writing more sophisticated, analytical paragraphs.

The MEAL Plan Paragraph Organization

In order to teach students how to structure a complex paragraph, some academic institutions offer the MEAL plan. On the next page, take a look at the same paragraph above with the MEAL plan labels.

M	Main Idea
E	Evidence
A	Analysis
L	Link back to main idea

MEAL Plan Paragraph Breakdown

MAIN IDEA: The student population within higher education is rapidly changing. Gone are the days of the ruddy faced freshmen leaving their homes to experience their first taste of independence without parental intervention or control. In contrast, today's college students are more experienced, slightly older, and academically challenged. **EVIDENCE:** In a Chronicle of Higher Education article, *Raising Graduation Rates Involves More Than Just Colleges*, Espinosa (2010) describes these 21st century learners as, "those from growing racial and ethnic minority groups, those who are the first in their families to attend college, adult learners, and displaced workers." **ANALYSIS:** Unfortunately, these millennial students are also products of a broken, chaotic public education system that has rendered them unprepared for college level curriculums. However, the current economic crisis demands that workers possess higher skill levels and college degrees in order to become successful in today's fast-paced, global workplaces. **LINK BACK:** As a result, more workers feel the pressure to enter college, and college institutions feel the pressure to accommodate students who are academically unprepared for college life.

Who Writes Complex Paragraphs?

Typically, K-6 students are not expected to write complex paragraphs as shown in this chapter. However, high school, college, and graduate students are expected to write these kinds of research-based paragraphs before entering an undergraduate or graduate school program. Remember, complex paragraphs are found in a variety of academic writing, such as research papers, reports, theses, dissertations, as well as professional or business writing.

Chapter Four
Reporter's Questions

Photo by Andrea Piacquadio from Pexels.

What are the Reporter's Questions?

As stated earlier, *The Five Ws and One H*—also referred to as *The Six Ws*—is a brainstorming technique. These are also called **reporter's questions**, because journalists are taught to provide information that answers these questions in the lead of a story. Without reading the entire article, the audience should understand the basic facts just by reading the very first paragraph.

The Five Ws and One H:
- Who?
- What?
- When?
- Where?
- Why?
- How?

In the workplace, the art of summary and brevity is an essential skill to master. Answering these reporter's questions before drafting a document drills down to its core ideas. As a result, the document will be focused, clear and concise. Furthermore, readers will not have to dig through excess verbiage to understand the main points of the document. A quick scan of the beginning of your business writing should satisfy a reader's need to gather important information quickly.

How to Use the Reporter's Questions

These questions help students to brainstorm and organize ideas for their essays before beginning to write the first draft. Write the six reporter's questions down on a sheet of paper. After considering the kind of assignment you need to write and its subject, write an answer to each question. Keep brainstorming and researching until you can adequately answer each question. If you still need assistance on how to apply this technique to your own writing, the following breakdown of each question should be helpful.

Who?

- Who is involved?
- Who is affected?
- Who will benefit?
- Who will be harmed?

What?

- What happened?
- What is your subject narrowed down to a simple phrase or sentence?
- What does your topic involve? What are the different parts to it?
- What is it similar to or different from?
- What might be affected or changed by your topic?

When?

- Day, month, year, date, time of day?
- When did the situation happen?
- Will the event take place in the future?
- Did the event happen in the past?
- Is there an important timeframe or deadline to mention?

Why?

- Why is this topic important?
- Why does it matter?
- Why do certain things happen?
- What are some causes and effects within the topic?

Where?

- Where did it take place?
- Where will it take place?
- Where should it take place?
- Does it matter where it takes place?
- Is the situation affected by location?

How?

- How does this process work?
- How does it function?
- How did it come to be?
- How are those involved affected?

Knowledge Check

1. What is the maximum word length for sentences?

2. How many sentences are in a mid-length paragraph?

3. What is the active voice?

4. What is the first step of the writing process?

5. What prewriting technique consists of circles?

6. What step of the writing process does proofreading fall under?

7. How many steps are in the writing process?

Answers: **1.** 15-20 sentences **2.** 5-7 sentences **3.** the verb is simple past or present and comes after the subject **4.** exploring ideas **5.** clustering **6.** step six-producing the final copy **7.** six

Reporter's Questions Exercise

Directions: Read the memo below. Based on the content of the memo, write out the answers to the six reporter's questions.

To: Michael West
CC: Colin Hinton

Subject: Management Training Proposal for John Walker Enterprises

Dear Michael,

It was good to see you yesterday at the weekly Marketing Manager's Round-up. This message is to confirm the direction we will take with the training proposal and to confirm the points we agreed upon.

As we discussed, you will continue to work on the technical aspects of the proposal, paying particular attention to the detailed points that Colin raised yesterday.

I will continue to work on the financial details. We agreed that I should consider the feasibility of a reduction in our fee rate for this client.

We both agreed to complete the first draft of this proposal by March 31. Once the draft is completed, I will send it to our administrative specialist, Tracy, to print and send to you and Colin through internal mail.

Okay, if you have further questions, let me know.

Regards,

Mac Mason, Director of Contracts

---

1. Who_____

2. What_____

3. When_____

4. Why_____

5. Where_____

6. How_____

Answers: Reporter's Questions Exercise

1. **Who:** Michael West, Colin Hinton, Mac Mason

2. **What:** Management Training Proposal for John Walker Enterprises

3. **When:** Yesterday; by March 31

4. **Why:** To confirm the direction we will take with the training proposal and to confirm the agreed upon points

5. **Where:** Marketing Manager's Round-up

6. **How:** Through internal mail

Chapter Five
Expository Writing: Narration

Photo by Cottonbros from Pexels.

What is Narration?

Narration is an expository writing technique that can be used in almost any writing assignment for a variety of reasons. In fact, storytelling is a hot social media marketing and branding strategy, because most people like to read a good story.

Key Points for Narration:

- Narration tells a story that explains what happened, when it happened, and who was involved.

- The narration should have a clear point.

- The narration should reveal what you want the reader to learn or take away from the story.

- A narration is not a short story, but an anecdote that still requires a beginning, middle, and end.

More Key Points for Narration:

- Remember, your narration needs to serve a purpose. Why are you sharing this story? What can readers learn from your experience? Make the point of the story known in its conclusion.

- Make sure all events in the narrative are told in a clear sequence, which is characteristic of good chronological order.

- Outline or jot down the events of your story before beginning to write.

- Use detailed descriptions and rich, colorful language to make your story vivid for the reader.

- Narration ends with a life lesson, inspirational takeaway or a call to action for the reader.

- Narration tells a story about an event or situation in chronological order from beginning to end.

What is Chronological Order?

Chronological order refers to arranging actions or events by time sequence starting with the earliest activity and ending with the last. For example, imagine that you are creating a meeting agenda. Susan Barlow speaks at 4 p.m. and Michael Gasson speaks at 10:00 a.m. You would put Michael before Susan on the agenda, because he speaks at an earlier time. Also, think of historical events which are also recalled by timeframe. Chronological order is also called linear or sequential order.

Key Points for Chronological Order:

- Narrative examples are told in chronological order, from beginning to end.

- Remember, narrative examples or stories have a beginning, middle and an end.

- As a beginning business writer, use a straightforward organizational structure. Avoid using flashbacks.

Transitional Words and Phrases

Since narration relies on chronological order or time sequence, phrases that signal time are helpful to the reader. For the sake of sentence variety, transitional words can appear at the beginning, middle or end of a sentence. Following are some of the most common transitions found in narrations.

Examples of Narrative Transitional Words and Phrases:

- after that
- afterward
- currently
- dates of the year
- eventually
- finally
- first

- meanwhile
- next
- now
- soon
- then
- time of day

Narrative Topic Sentence or Lead-in

Narrations often use implied thesis statements or topic sentences. Implied means that the direction of the story is suggested, not explicitly stated. Basically, before launching into a narrative example, you need a setup or a lead-in.

Examples:

- When I had trouble with my finances, help came from an unexpected source.
- The annual women's month celebration began in 2011 with Norma Cross in the public relations department.

Chronological Order Exercise

Directions: Number the sentences in order from 1-4.

Topic Sentence: A combination of talent and hard work has propelled Alicia Keys to musical stardom.

___In 1988, seven-year-old Alicia dazzled her first piano teacher by mastering classical and jazz pieces.

___By 2005, her distinctive voice and musical flair won a huge fan base and four more Grammys.

___As a teenager in the "Hell's Kitchen" section of New York City, she wrote her first songs and blossomed as a pianist.

___At age twenty, she released *Songs in A Minor*, the debut album that scored five Grammy awards in 2002.

Answers: Chronological Order Exercise

Topic Sentence: A combination of talent and hard work has propelled Alicia Keys to musical stardom.

1 In 1988, seven-year-old Alicia dazzled her first piano teacher by mastering classical and jazz pieces.

4 By 2005, her distinctive voice and musical flair won a huge fan base and four more Grammys.

2 As a teenager in the "Hell's Kitchen" section of New York City, she wrote her first songs and blossomed as a pianist.

3 At age twenty, she released *Songs in A Minor*, the debut album that scored five Grammy awards in 2002.

Narration Paragraph Example

Last September, I watched my ten-year-old grandson act like an adult in an emergency. While cleaning the living room carpet, I tripped and fell over the vacuum cleaner hose. At first, I was dazed. Soon, I realized that my left arm hurt terribly. I called to my grandson Joel, who was the only other person at home. When Joel saw me on the floor, his face went pale. Then he calmly took charge of the situation. He went to the phone and dialed for emergency help. I heard him give our address, exact details of what had happened, and a description of the position I was lying in. I could tell that he was carefully listening to the instructions he was given. Returning to the living room, Joel covered me with a wool blanket and told me that an ambulance was on its way. He sat by my side in the ambulance and stayed with me while the doctor treated me. My sprained arm bothered me for only three weeks, but I will always feel proud of what my grandson did on that day.

Key Points:

- Other than serving as an interesting conversation piece, this brief narrative example could be inserted into a grant proposal for giving CPR training to elementary school children.

- Notice how the first sentence serves as a lead-in.

- The narration technique can be used in a variety of situations and documents to add detail and interest to your writing.

Narration Exercise

Directions: First, delete the sentence with irrelevant details. Next, using the numbers 1-4, put all of the remaining sentences in order, starting with the next sentence that should follow the very first topic sentence. The goal is to arrange a logical, cohesive narration paragraph.

Topic Sentence:

Through talent and fortunate timing, Vera Wang has become one of the world's top designers of women's gowns.

_____ In 1971, after college, Wang became a fashion editor at *Vogue*, a job she held for fifteen years.

_____ Soon, stars like Halle Berry, Uma Thurman, and Meg Ryan began wearing Vera Wang gowns, and Wang's reputation soared.

_____ In 1990, Wang made her dream a reality, opening a high-style bridal and evening gown business.

_____ Every year, 2.4 million couples get married in the United States, spending an average of $19,000 per wedding.

_____ The world took note when Wang designed elegant costumes for skater Nancy Kerrigan during the much-watched 1994 Winter Olympics.

Answers: Narration Exercise

Topic Sentence:

Through talent and fortunate timing, Vera Wang has become one of the world's top designers of women's gowns.

___1___ In 1971, after college, Wang became a fashion editor at *Vogue*, a job she held for fifteen years.

___4___ Soon, stars like Halle Berry, Uma Thurman, and Meg Ryan began wearing Vera Wang gowns, and Wang's reputation soared.

___2___ In 1990, Wang made her dream a reality, opening a high-style bridal and evening gown business.

_____ ~~Every year, 2.4 million couples get married in the United States, spending an average of $19,000 per wedding.~~

___3___ The world took note when Wang designed elegant costumes for skater Nancy Kerrigan during the much-watched 1994 Winter Olympics.

Chapter Six

Expository Writing: Description

Photo by Fauxels from Canstock Photo.

What is Description?

Description tells what something—(a person, place, or thing)—looks like, feels like, sounds like, smells like, or tastes like. Basically, description relies on the five senses to create visual images for the reader. Just as a reminder, the five senses include: sight, hearing, taste, touch, and smell.

Key Points for Description:

- Descriptions use colorful language to highlight nouns. Nouns are people, places, things, or personified abstract ideas.

- Description uses the five senses to create visual images for the reader.

- Description essays usually focus on one specific person, place, thing, or event.

Objective Description

Objective description focuses on the object itself rather than your personal reactions to it. The example below offers a simple observation.

Example:

- a chair in the classroom

Objective descriptions use precise, factual observations without hinting at the writer's personal attitudes about the subject being described. In the example below, a wedding ring is being described according to its factual meaning in the dictionary.

Example:

- **wedding ring (n):** "a ring, usually of gold, platinum, or silver, given by one partner to the other during a marriage ceremony."

Subjective Description

Subjective description expresses an emotional response, personal opinion, or reaction to what is being described. The example below suggests an aversion to the object being described.

Example:

- slick, slimy, grasshopper green okra

Subjective descriptions use creative, more detailed writing—like figures of speech—and also include personal observations and emotions.

Example:

- "Lena cried as she removed her wedding ring; the symbol of her personal failure as a wife and mother."

Figures of Speech

The description technique often incorporates illustrative, unique language to enhance the reader's understanding of your writing. Although **figures of speech** are most often used in fiction, poetry or literature, these devices can also boost your academic writing.

Simile: a non-literal comparison or association of two dissimilar things using the words *"like"* or *"as."*

Simile Example:

- "free as a bird"

Metaphor: a non-literal comparison or association of two different things without using the words *like* or *as*.

Example:

- "The school computers are old dinosaurs."

Personification: giving human attributes to inanimate objects.

Example:

- "The wind whispered the names of the dead across the plains."

Allusion: a historical, cultural or religious reference that the writer assumes the readers will recognize.

Example:

- "The teacher towered over the student like Goliath over David."

Description Paragraph Example

The woman who met us had an imposing beauty. She was tall and large-boned. Her face was strongly molded, with high cheekbones and skin the color of mahogany. She greeted us politely, but did not smile and seemed to hold her head very high, an effect exaggerated by an abundance of black hair slicked up and rolled on the top of her head. Her clothing was simple, a black sweater and skirt, and I remember thinking that dressed in showier garments, this woman would have been breathtaking.

Key Points:

- **Dominant Impression** is the mood or feeling the reader senses after reading a description. How should your readers feel after reading your writing?

- **Vantage Point** is what the observer sees from a particular position. What can you see while looking at an object straight on? From behind? From the left or from the right?

- **Spatial Order** refers to how things are positioned in an environment, such as *to the left of the front door*.

Selection of Descriptive Details

- Give specific details when appropriate, instead of writing general, bland prose.

- Do not go overboard in loading your sentences or paragraphs with excessive detail.

- Avoid details that are minor or unimportant to the story.

- Give just enough vivid detail to help the reader create a mental picture of what is being written about.

Sensory Description Example:

The thick, burnt scent of roasted coffee tickled the tip of my nose just seconds before the old, faithful alarm blared a distorted top-forty through its tiny top speaker. Wiping away the grit of last night's sleep, the starch white sunlight blinded me momentarily as I slung my arm like an elephant trunk along the top of the alarm, searching for the snooze button. While stretching hands and feet to the four posts of my bed, my eyes opened after several watery blinks. I crawled out of the comforter, edging awkwardly like a butterfly from a cocoon, swinging my legs over the side of the bed. The dusty pebbles on the chilled, wood floor sent ripples spiraling from my ankles to the nape of my neck when my feet hit the floor. Grabbing the apricot, terry-cloth robe, recently bathed in fabric softener and October wind, I knotted it tightly at my waist like a prestigious coat of armor and headed downstairs to battle the morning.

- Is this too much description?

- Can any details be deleted without changing the meaning of the paragraph?

- What details would you add or delete?

Description Exercise

Directions: Read the paragraph and answer the questions that follow.

(1) One look at my dog reveals that she has a mixed background. (2) Her long tapered nose is like those of German shepherds or collies. (3) On either side of her black head are small, folded-over ears like those of a terrier. (4) The fur around her neck is soft and thick, but on her back, it's short like a dachshund's. (5) All over her body, her white coat is covered with black spots. (6) Some are large, like a beagle's, and some are very small and close together, like the spots on a Dalmatian. (7) Her tail is long and hairy, just like a golden retriever's.

1. Give the number of the topic sentence that states the overall impression of the subject. _____

2. How are the details in this paragraph arranged?

    a. front to back

    b. near to far

    c. outside to inside

Directions: Following is a topic sentence followed by supporting details. Arrange this group of descriptive details in logical spatial order from 1-5.

3. Describe an old bike.

_____ wide seat, adjustable in height

_____ nearly bald front tire, with inner tube of soft rubber

_____ scratched handlebars, with bell and rake levers

_____ back tire nearly flat

_____ pedals fixed to the chain wheel

Directions: Find the **irrelevant detail** and circle its letter.

4. On the plate lay an unappetizing hamburger.

    a. burned bun, black on the edges

    b. the burger cost two dollars

    c. fat dripping from the hamburger onto the plate

    d. parts of burger uncooked and partially frozen

    e. sour smell of the meat

Answers: Description Exercise

1. **(1)**

2. **(a) – front to back**

3. Describe an old bike.

*Logical order = top-to-bottom

___**2**___ wide seat, adjustable in height
___**4**___ nearly bald front tire, with inner tube of soft rubber
___**1**___ scratched handlebars, with bell and rake levers
___**5**___ back tire nearly flat
___**3**___ pedals fixed to the chain wheel

4. **(b) – the burger cost two dollars**

Chapter Seven

Expository Writing: Illustration

Photo by Christina Morillo from Pexels.

What is Illustration?

Illustration explains a general statement, topic, or idea with one or more specific examples by use of drawings or artwork. Through writing, you are creating visual images with words. Consider your social circles, academic and employment surroundings, the media, or personal experience as sources of examples.

Key Points for Illustration:

- Illustration explains a general principle or idea by using a number of well-chosen examples.
- Each illustrative example must relate to and support the general statement or topic of your writing project.
- In everyday writing, illustration is commonly used in speeches, sales or other types of presentations, because it enhances explanations of complex ideas by using relatable examples or visual graphics.

- Choose the best examples to illustrate your point.

- Do not overuse examples in your writing.

- Use 1-3 quality illustrative examples in your essay.

- Make your illustrative examples specific and descriptive.

- Use enough detail in your examples to make your point clear and vivid to the reader.

- Remember, since illustration adds further explanation, your audience must understand your examples and not be confused by them.

Transitional Words and Phrases

Because illustration adds further explanation and comprehension, illustrative examples usually follow introductory statements or lead-in sentences. So, they often appear in the middle or end of a written passage or presentation. Therefore, it is helpful to signal to your audience that additional explanatory information is coming next.

Examples of Illustrative Transitional Words and Phrases:

- for example
- another instance of
- for instance
- another example of
- here are a few examples

- also
- furthermore
- in other words
- to illustrate

Illustration Paragraph Example

Great athletes do not reach the top by talent alone, but by pushing themselves to the limit and beyond. For instance, basketball sensation Lebron James keeps striving to improve. Branded the next Michael Jordan when he was in high school and drafted by the Cleveland Cavaliers, James kept his cool and kept working hard. He emerged an All-Star and leader who propelled the Cavaliers to the NBA playoffs three years in a row and his 2008 Olympic teammates to a gold medal. James perfected his agility, strength, and health routines, even off-season. Another example is record-breaking swimmer, Dara Torres. After winning nine medals at four Olympic Games and becoming a mother at age 39, this racer continued to build power and speed with brutal daily workouts: 90 minutes each of hard swimming and strength training, plus two hours of stretching. At 41, the *oldest female swimmer ever to compete in the Olympics, Dara scored three more silver medals. Few players in any sport, however, can match the work ethic of Lance Armstrong. In 1996, this bicycle racer was diagnosed with testicular cancer that had spread to his brain and lungs. After surgery and chemotherapy left him weak and exhausted, Armstrong began a strict diet and training regimen, cycling up to six hours a day. His commitment paid off when he won the Tour de France, cycling's toughest race, seven years in a row. Armstrong retired in 2005, but at age 37, he announced that Dara Torres had inspired him to compete again. Like many top athletes, he turned his talent into greatness through sheer hard work.*

Key Points:

- What main idea did the above examples illustrate?
- How many examples are used to develop the main idea?
- Notice that each example clearly relates to the main idea.

Knowledge Check

Directions: Each general statement is followed by several examples. Circle the letter of the example that does <u>not</u> clearly illustrate the general statement.

1. **Many people are lively and creative in old age.**
   a. Eighty-seven-year-old Mary Baker Eddy founded *The Christian Science Monitor*, one of the world's greatest newspapers.
   b. Pablo Picasso was engraving and drawing at ninety.
   c. When she was 100 years of age, Grandma Moses was still painting.
   d. Madonna's albums still topped the charts when she was thirty-five.

2. **Communication tools designed to make us more productive often distract us and actually *reduce* our efficiency.**
   a. Throughout the day, we allow incoming e-mail messages to constantly interrupt us by reading them immediately.
   b. Television takes up too much of our free time; the average person now watches more than four hours per day.
   c. Ringing cell phones often interrupt us and pull our attention away from the task at hand.
   d. The ding of an instant message usually causes us to drop what we're doing to respond.

3. **My boss seems to go out of his way to make me miserable.**
   a. He waits until 4:45 p.m. and then runs to my desk with ten letters that "must be out tonight."
   b. He golfs every weekend.
   c. Last Friday, he backed his car into mine and ripped my fender.
   d. He allows me vacation time only in the coldest months of the year.

Answers: 1. (d) 2. (b) 3. (b)

Illustration Exercise

Directions: Read the paragraph and answer the questions below.

(1) Miniaturized versions of many products are now available to consumers. (2) The pocket PC, for instance, is a popular product in the small-scale craze. (3) This tiny computer can be carried in a shirt pocket or purse. (4) Taking up just 4 to 6 inches of space, it has a screen about the size of a playing card. (5) Yet, it can do almost everything a full-size laptop or desktop computer can do. (6) Users can send and receive e-mail, surf the internet, play games, listen to audio files, and store information, all with a handheld, wireless device. (7) Some models even include a telephone or camera. (8) Although using thumbs to type a message on a tiny keypad can slow down composition, this small but powerful gadget allows busy people to fire off messages or find online information no matter where they are.

1. Give the number of the topic sentence in the paragraph above.

    ----

2. How many examples does the writer use to develop the topic sentence? _____

3. Give the number of the sentence containing a transitional expression that introduces an illustration. _____

Directions: Circle the letter of the example that does not clearly illustrate the general statement.

4. **Radio and television personalities sometimes make amusing slips of the tongue when they are on the air.**

    a. One radio announcer said: "If you don't like the way you look, just visit a plastered surgeon."

    b. A talk-show host broke for a commercial with "We'll be right back after these words from General Fools."

    c. A slip of the tongue that seems to reveal the speaker's hidden feelings or thoughts is called a Freudian slip.

    d. A radio psychologist told listeners, "The happiest people are always those who wake up every morning with a porpoise."

Answers: Illustration Exercise

1. **(1)**

2. **(1)** – the pocket PC

3. **(2)**

4. **(c)**

Chapter Eight

Expository Writing: Definition

Photo by fizkes from Canstock Photo.

What is Definition?

Definition clarifies an unfamiliar word or concept beyond the dictionary definition. Some words are objective and easy to define in one sentence. Other concepts require more extensive examples to define, such as injustice or racism. In essays, definitions go beyond the dictionary meaning of a word. Many examples of definition illustrate the meaning of a word in a way that is contrary to its common definition or perception. Remember, this expository technique usually focuses on words with multiple meanings, perspectives, or emotional responses.

Key Points for Definition:

- **Definition** essays challenge readers to look at certain words or concepts in uncommon, enlightening, or creative ways to educate them or to change their perspective.

- **Definition** clearly defines an unfamiliar word or concept beyond the dictionary definition.

- **Definition** challenges readers to look at certain words or concepts in uncommon, enlightening, or creative ways.

- **Definition** often uses a combination of expository techniques—(narration, illustration and description)—to effectively present the main idea of the word being defined.

- There are **three types of definition**: synonym, class, and negation.

Definition by Synonym

A **synonym** is an easier, more familiar word that means the same thing as the word you are defining. This **definition by synonym** technique defines an unfamiliar word by providing a synonym with the same part of speech as the original word.

Examples:

- **Gregarious** (adj.) means to be **sociable.**

- **Procrastinate** (v.) means to **postpone**.

- **Temerity** (n.) means **boldness**.

Definition by Class

Defining a word by class means putting it into a larger category (or class), and providing its distinguishing characteristics. **Definition by class** is two-fold. First, you place the word into a larger category or class. Second, you provide the distinguishing characteristics or details that make the person, place or thing being defined different from all others in that category.

Examples:

Word	Category/Class	Distinguishing Details
• lemonade	beverage	lemon, sugar, water
• laptop	computer	light, mobile, small
• psychiatrist	medical doctor	specializes in mental and emotional illness

Definition by Negation

Definition by negation challenges preconceived notions of certain words and concepts. It defines a word by telling what it is **NOT**, then illustrating what it **IS** by presenting a different perspective.

Example:

- A **good parent** does not just feed and clothe a child, but unconditionally loves, accepts, and supports that child into adulthood.

Negation Paragraph Example

A *feminist* is not a man-hater, a masculine woman, a demanding shrew, or someone who dislikes housewives. A feminist is simply a woman (or a man) who believes that women should enjoy the same rights, privileges, opportunities, and compensation as men. Today, feminists want women to receive equal pay for equal work. They support a woman's right to pursue her goals and dreams, whether she wants to be an astronaut, athlete, banker, or homemaker. Because the term is often misunderstood, some people do not call themselves feminists, but share feminist values.

Key Points:

- What word is being defined?

- Can you spot any other expository techniques in this paragraph?

- Does this definition challenge your previous ideas about this word?

Definition Paragraph Example

Ambivalence can be defined as a feeling or attitude that is both positive and negative at the same time. For instance, a young woman might feel ambivalent about motherhood. She may want to have a child yet fear that motherhood will use up energy she would like to spend on her career. A Michigan man who is offered a slightly higher salary in Arizona might be ambivalent about moving. He and his family don't want to leave their friends, their schools, and a city they love. On the other hand, they are tempted by a larger income and by Arizona's warm climate and clean air. Finally, two people may have ambivalent feelings about each other, loving and disliking each other at the same time. It hurts to be together, and it hurts to be apart; neither situation makes them happy. As these examples show, the double tug of ambivalence can complicate decision making.

Key Points:

- What word is being defined?

- How many illustrative examples are used to define this word?

- How many expository techniques can you spot in this paragraph?

Where are the Essay Examples?

So far, this book has focused on providing paragraph examples for each expository technique instead of full essays. Why? Because students should create their own work without lifting papers off of the internet or buying one from a seedy essay broker. If you understand the techniques as presented in each chapter, then you should be able to write a paragraph similar to the examples. If you can write a short paragraph essay of 10-12 sentences, then you can expand that into a two or three-page essay.

Remember, every assignment will have a beginning, middle, and an end—or—an introduction, body, and conclusion, regardless of the expository technique you are using to build your essay. So, the general essay structure remains the same as illustrated below. Some call it the five-paragraph essay structure. Although most essays extend beyond five paragraphs, this is still a handy organizational structure to remember, especially for novice writers.

INTRODUCTION	• Gives the background information necessary to understand the main idea of the entire essay. • Ends with a thesis statement.
BODY	**Topic Sentence #1** Supporting sentences and examples
	Topic Sentence #2 Supporting sentences and examples
	Topic Sentence #3 Supporting sentences and examples
CONCLUSION	• Summarizes the main three points in the body of the essay. • Ends with a universal lesson, something to consider, or a call to action.

Definition Exercise

Directions: Identify each of the following definitions as a **synonym definition**, **class definition**, or **definition by negation**. Circle the letter of the correct answer.

1. A yak is an ox that is large and long-haired, and it is found wild or domesticated in Tibet.

    a. synonym definition

    b. class definition

    c. definition by negation

2. Multitasking means doing more than two things at the same time.

    a. synonym definition

    b. class definition

    c. definition by negation

3. An essay is not just a padded paragraph, but a short composition that develops more ideas about a topic.

    a. synonym definition

    b. class definition

    c. definition by negation

Answers: Definition Exercise

1. **(b)** class definition

2. **(a)** synonym definition

3. **(c)** definition by negation

Chapter Nine
Expository Writing: Process

Photo by fizkes from Canstock Photo.

What is Process?

Quite simply, **process** tells how to do something by listing specific steps in chronological order from first to last. In the workplace, you might need to tell the school staff members how to create a signature block at the bottom of their outgoing emails. Your explanation takes the form of a process as you walk them through the steps to perform this action. In addition to this *how-to* format, process techniques can be used to explain activity that cannot be performed, but merely understood.

For example, you can explain childbirth from conception to delivery, but you cannot perform the activity happening within a woman's womb. You can explain the stages of growth that the fetus endures, but you cannot put your hands to them and perform them yourself. So, there are two types of process: 1) **directional** or *how-to* 2) **operational** or explanatory. The first email example is directional, and the second on childbirth is operational.

Key Points for Process:

- All steps must be listed in the correct order from beginning to end.

- Process includes tips, which are special techniques that will improve or maximize the process or the product that is produced.

- Process also includes warnings, which are alerts of potential danger or harm if the process is not performed correctly.

- When writing process examples, it is good practice to introduce tips and warnings to the reader as soon as possible.

Directional Process

A **directional process** (how-to) can be directly performed. You might be familiar with this type of process through how-to articles and videos, or food recipes. Social media is replete with information on how to create or complete something. A directional process also includes ingredients, equipment or tools needed to finish a task or assignment.

Directional Paragraph Example:

Careful preparation before an interview is the key to getting the job you want. The first step is to learn all you can about the employer. Research and read about the company. You can find company websites and other useful information online. Second, as you read, think about the ways your talents match the company's goals. Third, put yourself in the interviewer's place, and make a list of questions that he or she will probably ask. Employers want to know about your experience, training, and special skills. Remember, every employer looks for a capable and enthusiastic team player who will help the firm succeed. Fourth, rehearse your answers to the questions out loud. Practice with a friend or record yourself, until your responses sound well prepared and confident. Finally, select a professional looking interview outfit well in advance to avoid last minute panic. When you, as a job candidate, make the effort to prepare, the interviewer will likely be impressed.

Operational Process

An **operational process** (explanatory) explains and describes the steps and stages of an activity. Usually, an operational process cannot be directly performed, such as natural weather events. For example, you cannot create a flood, but you can explain how flooding occurs in a certain region. However, some topics can be written from both a directional and an operational perspective. For example, recovery from addiction can be explained, but this process also contains steps that can be performed.

Directional Paragraph Example:

Many experts believe that recovery from addiction, whether to alcohol or other drugs, has four main stages. The first stage begins when the user finally admits that he or she has a substance abuse problem and wants to quit. At this point, most people seek help from groups like Alcoholics Anonymous or other treatment programs because few addicts can "get clean" by themselves. The next stage is withdrawal when the addict stops using the substance. Withdrawal can be a painful physical and emotional experience, but luckily, it does not last long. After withdrawal comes the most challenging stage—making positive life changes. Recovering addicts have to learn new ways of spending their time, finding pleasure and relaxation, caring for their bodies, and relating to spouses, family, and friends. The fourth and final stage is staying off drugs. This open-ended part of the process often calls for ongoing support or therapy. For people once defeated by addiction, the rewards of self-esteem and a new life are well worth the effort.

Imperative Statements

Process examples often use sentences written with an understood "you," or an **imperative statement**. The first statement below is not imperative, but the second example statement becomes imperative by deleting "you."

Example:

- First, **you** pour cold root beer over the ice cream.
- First, pour cold root beer over the ice cream.

Key Points

- Imperative statements are commands and are used to give direction.
- Instead of repeating "you" throughout the document, write sentences using the imperative format.
- The subject of the understood "you" is the person performing the action.

Transitional Words and Phrases

Much like narration, process flows according to chronological order or linear sequence. Since process relies on sequence, words and phrases that signal a change in step or stage are helpful to the reader. This is particularly important, because a misstep could cause a critical or fatal mistake. For the sake of sentence variety, transitional words can appear at the beginning, middle or end of a sentence. Following are some of the most common transitions found in process examples.

Examples of Process Transitional Words and Phrases:

- after
- at first
- before
- begin by
- during
- finally
- first, second, third...
- initially

- last
- later
- meanwhile
- next
- then
- until
- when
- while

Identifying Transitions Exercise

Directions: Write all of the transitional words and phrases from this paragraph in the blanks below.

You should first get out four hamburger buns. Second, spread mustard on top of each bun. Third, put a slice of turkey and a slice of Swiss cheese in each bun. Then, wrap each bun in a sheet of aluminum foil. Next, put the sandwiches on a baking sheet and put them in a 350-degree oven for 20 minutes. Finally, remove the sandwiches from the oven and serve them piping hot.

_____

_____

_____

Answers: Identifying Transitions Exercise

You should **first** get out four hamburger buns. **Second,** spread mustard on top of each bun. **Third,** put a slice of turkey and a slice of Swiss cheese in each bun. **Then**, wrap each bun in a sheet of aluminum foil. **Next**, put the sandwiches on a baking sheet and put them in a 350-degree oven for 20 minutes. **Finally,** remove the sandwiches from the oven and serve them piping hot.

List of Transition Answers:

- first, second

- third, then

- next, finally

Process Paragraph Example

You are sitting in a restaurant quietly having a meal when suddenly a man nearby starts choking on a piece of food lodged in his throat. By using the Heimlich maneuver, you may be able to save this person's life. Your two hands are all you need to perform this lifesaving technique. First, position yourself behind the choking person. Then wrap your arms around the person's midsection, being careful not to apply any pressure to the chest or stomach. Once your arms are around the victim, clench one hand into a fist and cup this fist in the other hand. Now turn the fist so that the clenched thumb points toward the spot between the choker's navel and midsection. Finally, thrust inward at this spot using a quick, sharp motion. If this motion does not dislodge the food, repeat it until the victim can breathe freely.

Key Points:

- How many steps are described in this process?

- How many transitional words can you find?

- How many imperative statements can you count?

Process Exercise #1

Directions: Read the paragraph and answer the questions that follow.

(1) Anyone can conquer clutter by following a series of steps. (2) First of all, pick just one area on which to focus your attention. (3) This might be a shelf, a closet, or even just one drawer. (4) Second, round up some bags or boxes and label them so that you have one of each of the following: *Repair, Relocate, Donate, Sell, Store, Throw Away,* and *Return.* (5) Next, sort all of the items in the area by placing them in one of the bags or boxes, depending on what needs to happen to it. (6) Then, take action on each pile. (7) Put *Repair, Donate,* and *Return* items in your car so that you can drop them off on your next errand run; take the items in the *Relocate* box to the places where they belong; toss out the *Throw Away* items; etc. (8) Finally, clean your newly decluttered area and give yourself a reward for a job well done!

1. Give the number of the topic sentence in the paragraph above.
   _____

2. How many steps are in the process? _____

3. List the transitional expressions in the paragraph that locate the steps of the process in time:

   _____

   _____

   _____

   _____

   _____

   _____

Answers:
1. (1)   2. (5)   3. First of all (sentence 2); Second (sentence 4); Next (sentence 5); Then (sentence 6); Finally (sentence 8)

Process Exercise #2

Directions: Read the paragraph and answer the questions that follow.

(1) Learning to make a budget is the key to managing your hard-earned money. (2) First, select your budget period, usually a week or a month. (3) Second, estimate your income for that time period as accurately as you can. (4) Include not only your salary after payroll deductions, but the least you expect to make from other sources, such as tips, bonuses, and commissions. (5) Third, add up all your expenses for the budget period. (6) Be sure to add in your fixed costs—like rent, utilities, tuition, and taxes—as well as savings. (7) Also include your variable expenses. (8) The most difficult ones to estimate—variable expenses—include all your nonfixed living costs, from money for food and transportation to planned events like vacations and less predictable ones like medical and home repair bills. (9) Fourth, subtract your expenses from your income to see whether you need to adjust your budget. (10) If your expenses are greater than your income, look for ways to cut costs—for example, on clothing. (11) If your income is greater than your expenses, you have the luxury of splurging or saving extra money for that car or trip you have always wanted.

1. Give the number of the topic sentence in the paragraph above. _____

2. How many steps are in the process? _____

3. List the transitional expressions in the paragraph that identify the steps of the process:

   _____
   _____
   _____

Directions: Cross out the irrelevant detail. Number all remaining statements in logical chronological order.

4. **Ted learned business skills in stages throughout his life.**
   _____ He took several sales and marketing courses in college.
   _____ As a child after school, he watched his parents run their candy shop.
   _____ When he was twenty-eight years old, he married his college girlfriend.
   _____ Finally, he opened his own T-shirt store in the mall after graduation.
   _____ In high school, he spent afternoons selling shoes at his uncle's store.
   _____ In his senior year, Ted made excellent money selling health products out of his home.

Answers: Process Exercise #2

1. (1)

2. (4)

3. **First** (sentence 2)
   Second (sentence 3)
   Third (sentence 5)
   Fourth (sentence 9)

4. **Ted learned business skills in stages throughout his life.**

   ___**4**___ He took several sales and marketing courses in college.

   ___**1**___ As a child after school, he watched his parents run their candy shop.

   _____ ~~When he was twenty-eight years old, he married his college girlfriend.~~

   ___**5**___ Finally, he opened his own T-shirt store in the mall after graduation.

   ___**2**___ In high school, he spent afternoons selling shoes at his uncle's store.

   ___**3**___ In his senior year, Ted made excellent money selling health products out of his home.

Chapter Ten
Expository Writing:
Comparison and Contrast

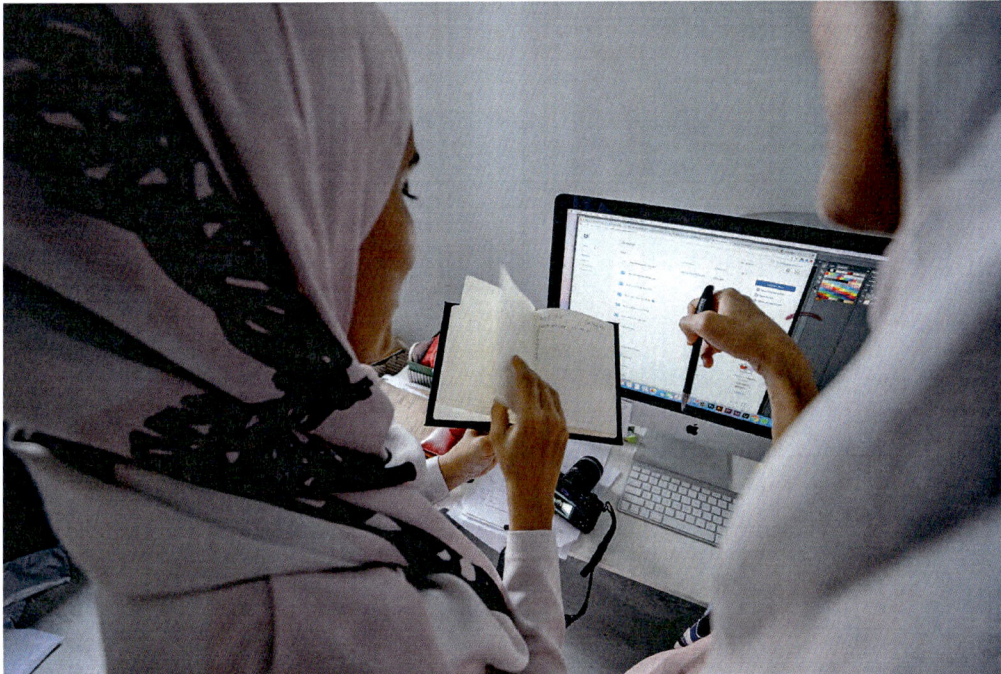

Photo by Mentatdgt from Pexels.

What is Comparison and Contrast?

Comparison and Contrast is an expository technique that analyzes similarities and differences. Comparison finds the similarities between two things. Contrast focuses on the differences between two things. In the workplace, you might need to present the total number of textbook sales from the last two years to see if sales have increased or decreased and why. You can see how charts comparing and contrasting the two might be helpful in discovering opportunities for success in textbook sales. In fact, we use this technique in everyday life whenever we compare product prices and brands to get the better value before making a purchase. A simple item such as toilet paper requires less investigation than choosing the right health insurance plan that cannot be changed until the next year. Therefore, comparison and contrast encourages critical thinking and close examination before making decisions.

Key Points for Comparison/Contrast:

- The two items being compared or contrasted need to be of the same category. For example, you can compare or contrast dogs and cats, because both are domesticated animals.

- Comparison and contrast are often used together to express complex, critical thought and organizational processes.

- Documents or short examples that use comparison and contrast must be organized effectively.

- Choose an identifiable structure before writing.

- Points of comparison or contrast must be parallel between both subjects.

- Depending on your topic and purpose, you might need to use comparison only without contrast or vice versa. You might also only focus on contrast without comparison.

Points of Comparison and Contrast

Whether you choose to compare or contrast, you must decide what qualities, characteristics or details to base your analysis on. For example, if you were choosing between two computer printers, you might look at price, size and cartridge type. These are your points of comparison and contrast.

To keep your thoughts organized, you might develop a chart or table like the one below:

PRINTER A	PRINTER B
price	price
size	size
cartridge type	cartridge type

Subject-by-Subject Structure

Instead of comparing two distinct items, you might take two general subjects, and break them down by specific points of comparison or contrast. Your two subjects might be television marketing and radio marketing. Notice that these two different types of marketing are in the same general category of media marketing. Your points of comparison could be men, women, and children. What is your purpose in analyzing these two kinds of media by these three points of comparison? Perhaps you want to know which audience is targeted the most on each medium.

Example of Subject-by-Subject Structure:

Subject A Television Marketing	Subject B Radio Marketing
Point 1: Men	**Point 1:** Men
Point 2: Women	**Point 2:** Women
Point 3: Children	**Point 3:** Children

Point-by-Point Structure

Instead of discussing all of one subject followed by all of the next subject, as in the subject-by-subject structure, you might need to use a structure that flows back and forth between the two subjects. The information is the same, but in this structure, the arrangement of the information is different.

Subject A: TV—Men, **Point 1**
Subject B: Radio—Men, **Point 1**
Subject A: TV—Women, **Point 2**
Subject B: Radio—Women, **Point 2**
Subject A: TV—Children, **Point 3**
Subject B: Radio—Children, **Point 3**

Key Words and Phrases

Unlike transitional words that appear within a sentence or paragraph, certain phrases or questions indicate that a comparison or contrast is necessary to adequately present the information that is being requested. See some of these examples below.

Examples of Comparison/Contrast Signal Phrases:

- advantages/disadvantages
- compare/contrast
- conversely, in contrast
- evaluate, yet
- however, likewise
- similarities/differences

- Where would you rather?
- Which do you prefer?
- Which is better?
- Which is easier?
- Which is more difficult?
- Which is more effective?

Comparison/Contrast Paragraph Example

Both a cold and the flu can make you miserable, but they are different in several ways. Experts say a cold will go away by itself. However, the flu can lead to pneumonia and other serious or even deadly problems. A cold usually comes on gradually, accompanied by little or no fever. In contrast, the flu comes on suddenly, and its fever can spike as high as 104 degrees and linger for three or four days. Someone with a cold might experience mild body aches and fatigue, but the flu often brings severe body aches, deep fatigue, chills, and a major headache. In general, a cold is wet, with much congestion, a runny nose, and even runny eyes. The flu, on the other hand, is far drier, marked by a dry cough.

Key Points:

- What two things are being compared and or contrasted?

- Does this paragraph compare, contrast, or both?

- Does this paragraph include any signal words or phrases?

Comparison/Contrast Exercise

Directions: Read the paragraphs and answer the questions that follow.

(1) The city of Bangalore, India, is a jarring mixture of traditional and modern living. (2) Bangalore has become a world center of the computer software industry, and companies like IBM, Dell, and Hewlett Packard have built dozens of gleaming new buildings. (3) In contrast, the rutted dirt roads are choked with oxcarts, and three-wheeled taxis belch black fumes. (4) Over breakfast each morning at the Taj Residency Hotel, Indian programmers chat with American engineers about the latest piece of computer code. (5) Yet, sandal-clad women carry baskets of tools on their heads at a nearby construction site, and workers drag a huge pipe into place using only ropes. (6) Each night, teams of programmers send their work by satellite uplink to teams on the other side of the earth. (7) However, they must rely on diesel generators because power outages lasting two or three hours occur almost every day.

1. Give the number of the topic sentence in the paragraph above. _____

2. Does this paragraph compare, contrast, or both?
    a. compares only
    b. contrasts only
    c. compares and contrasts

3. What two things are being compared and/or contrasted?
    _____
    _____

4. List the transitional expressions that indicate contrast or comparison:
    _____
    _____
    _____
    _____

Answers: Comparison/Contrast Exercise

1. **(1)**

2. **(b)**—contrasts only

3. traditional and modern living in Bangalore, India

4. **in contrast** (sentence 3); **yet** (sentence 5); **however** (sentence 7)

Chapter Eleven
Expository Writing:
Cause and Effect

Photo by Julia M Cameron from Pexels.

What is Cause and Effect?

Cause and effect essays examine the reasons a situation or event occurs, and the outcomes or results of that situation. There are several ways to organize a cause and effect document. Some organizational structures concentrate on causes while others might focus only on effects. Some topics require a combination of both. The key is to clearly discuss causes and effects without mixing them together or forgetting to give details for one or the other.

Key Points for Cause & Effect:

- Causes are the reasons why something happens.
- Effects are the results of an action or situation.

- Cause and effect techniques examine the reasons why something happens, and the outcomes or consequences that follow.

- In the workplace, cause and effect is often used when discussing or analyzing data, especially in sales reports. This technique is also useful for highlighting problems that might get worse if a particular solution is not enacted.

- Cause and effect is used to describe problems and offer solutions.

Defining Causes and Effects

When using this technique, it is important to correctly separate causes from effects. Since the two are intertwined, sometimes discussions involving both of them get blurred. It might be helpful to develop a chart like the one below to get clear before drafting a document.

What causes people to overeat?

- Stress
- Skipping meals
- Boredom

What are the effects of overeating?

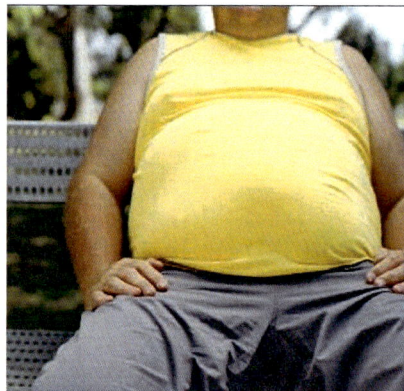

- Obesity
- Health problems
- Fatigue

Organizational Structures

The cause and effect technique offers similar options for organizational structures as comparison and contrast. You can likewise discuss causes only or effects only. For example, an entire research document can focus entirely on causes without mentioning effects. Since cause usually produces some type of effect, the two are generally presented together. Therefore, the following structures incorporate causes with effects.

Examples of Organizational Structures:

In the **subject-by-subject** pattern, all of the causes are discussed first followed by all of the effects. In the **point-by-point** arrangement, the main points of the causes and effects alternate.

SUBJECT-BY-SUBJECT	POINT-BY-POINT
• Cause 1	• Cause 1
• Cause 2	• Effect 1
• Cause 3	• Cause 2
• Effect 1	• Effect 2
• Effect 2	• Cause 3
• Effect 3	• Effect 3

Key Words and Phrases

Have you ever had to answer an open-ended question on a test, survey, or brief essay response? You might have noticed some of the words and phrases below that signal cause and effect.

Examples of Cause/Effect Signal Phrases:

SIGNAL WORDS FOR CAUSE	SIGNAL WORDS FOR EFFECT
• another factor	• another result
• explain why	• as a result
• because	• consequently
• give reasons why	• one important effect
• what is the cause of	• outcome
• results from	• the results of
• why	• what is the impact of

Cause/Effect Paragraph Example

(1) Why is the United States currently experiencing a serious shortage of registered nurses? (2) One reason for the problem is that many older nurses are retiring. (3) As they leave the profession, they leave many job openings behind them. (4) A second reason is declining enrollment at nursing schools across the country. (5) Fewer people are choosing to become nurses. (6) Consequently, positions are left unfilled. (7) Yet another reason for the shortage is the increased need for nursing services. (8) As the American population ages, more and more people need nursing services, not just in hospitals but in a variety of health-care settings. (9) Therefore, the number of nursing jobs is growing, but there aren't enough new recruits to staff them.

Key Points:

- Does this paragraph focus on cause, effect or both?
- How many causes can you identify? How many effects?
- Does this paragraph include any signal words or phrases?

1. Give the number of the topic sentence in the paragraph above. _____

2. How many causes or effects does the writer present? _____

3. List the transitional expressions in the paragraph that signal cause or effect:

Answers: 1. (1) 2. (3) 3. One reason (sentence 2), A second reason (sentence 4), Consequently (sentence 6), Yet another reason (sentence 7), Therefore (sentence 9)

Cause and Effect Exercise

Directions: On the blanks, write the cause and the effect contained in each of the following statements.

1. Natural disasters like hurricanes often cause the price of gasoline to rise.

Cause: _____

Effect: _____

2. Tom moved to Philadelphia because his employer transferred him there.

Cause: _____

Effect: _____

3. The high rate of divorce has increased the number of single-parent families in America.

Cause: _____

Effect: _____

4. Many people conquer their addiction to alcohol by joining the twelve-step Alcoholics Anonymous program.

Cause: _____

Effect: _____

5. The factory is adding a second shift and hiring more employees because orders have increased.

Cause: _____

Effect: _____

Answers: Cause and Effect Exercise

1. **Cause:** natural disasters like hurricanes

   Effect: price of gasoline rises

2. **Cause:** employer transferred him

   Effect: Tom moved to Philadelphia

3. **Cause:** high rate of divorce

   Effect: increase in the number of single-parent families in America

4. **Cause:** joining the twelve-step Alcoholics Anonymous program

   Effect: people conquer their addiction

5. **Cause:** orders have increased

   Effect: factory is adding a second shift and hiring more employees

Chapter Twelve
Expository Writing: Classification

Photo by Ekaterina Bolovtsova from Pexels.

What is Classification?

Classification helps make sense of the world by taking large amounts of information, and putting them into smaller categories based on one idea for division. The classification expository essay technique divides people, objects or ideas into separate groups. In general, each item is categorized according to **one standard** or one basis for dividing them.

Key Points for Classification:

- Classification divides people, objects or ideas into separate groups to illustrate their characteristics, differences or similarities.

- Classification uses serious or humorous writing styles to present categories in interesting or informative ways.

Examples of Classification

Classification requires you to identify what you are categorizing and how. The following examples of simple classification will help you understand how to divide more complex items according to more sophisticated criterion. As in the first example, the manner of separation and the standard for division might be the same. However, as the second example illustrates, you might need to subdivide a group by using a different standard or basis for division. You can also use numerous categories to further divide your subjects.

- **Object:** a bag of marbles
- **How to divide or separate them:** by color
- **Standard** (or basis) **for division:** color
- **Categories:** plain & glossy

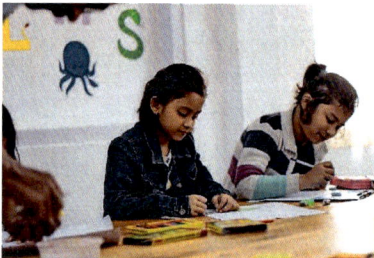

- **People:** elementary students
- **How to divide or separate them:** by grade
- **Standard** (or basis) **for division:** age
- **Categories: ages** 6-8 & 8-10

Classification Paragraph Example

Houseguests can be classified according to their level of self-sufficiency as independent, semi-dependent, or completely dependent. Independent guests make an effort to fit their routines to yours; they make their own beds, cook breakfast if they get up early, and know how to entertain themselves if you have other things to do. These usually are the guests you want to invite back. Semi-dependent guests demand more of your attention and companionship; they may want to be driven around town or may urge you to play pool with them even though you hate pool or have a term paper due. Still, the guests in this category may have charming qualities that make their visit worthwhile. Most infuriating are the helplessly dependent guests, who enter your house as if it were a hospital or spa, expecting to be taken care of. My friend George, for example, sprawls on a chair, his feet on my coffee table, complaining about his love life while I cook dinner, set the table, and change the CDs. After two days of waiting on George while I try to solve his problems, I'm exhausted. Overall, houseguests are a mixed blessing—some more mixed than others.

Key Points:

- How many categories appear in this passage?

- What are the names of the categories?

- What is the basis or standard for division?

Transitional Words and Phrases

Examples of Classification Transitional Words and Phrases:

- according to
- can be divided
- can be classified
- can be categorized

- the first type
- the second kind
- the last category
- types of

Classification: Important Reminders

- Remember, classification divides people, objects or ideas into separate groups to illustrate their characteristics, differences or similarities.

- To stay focused and clear, use only **one standard** or basis of division.

- **Narrow your categories** for effective classification. For example, TV viewers is too broad, so is male and female viewers. However, **couch potatoes broken into four categories**—avid, casual, wishy-washy, and last resort—is more narrow. The basis of comparison could be the number of hours spent per day on watching television.

- Illustrate the categories with examples.

- Avoid stereotypes that reinforce negative opinions or prejudice.

- Although you want to present information in interesting or informative ways, use a professional writing style and use humor sparingly or not at all to avoid offending someone.

Knowledge Check

Directions: Read the paragraph and answer the questions that follow.

(1) Houseguests can be classified according to their level of self-sufficiency as independent, semi-dependent, or completely dependent. (2) Independent guests make an effort to fit their routines to yours; they make their own beds, cook breakfast if they get up early, and know how to entertain themselves if you have other things to do. (3) These usually are the guests you want to invite back. (4) Semi-dependent guests demand more of your attention and companionship; they may want to be driven around town or may urge you to play pool with them even though you hate pool or have a term paper due. (5) Still, the guests in this category may have charming qualities that make their visit worthwhile. (6) Most infuriating are the helplessly dependent guests, who enter your house as if it were a hospital or spa, expecting to be taken care of. (7) My friend George, for example, sprawls on a chair, his feet on my coffee table, complaining about his love life while I cook dinner, set the table, and change the CDs. (8) After two days of waiting on George while I try to solve his problems, I'm exhausted. (9) As these categories show, houseguests are a mixed blessing—some more mixed than others.

1. Give the number of the topic sentence in the paragraph above. _____

2. How many categories are there?

   _____

3. List the categories from question #2.

4. On what basis does the writer classify houseguests?

Answers: 1. (1)   2. (3)   3. level of self-sufficiency   4. independent, semi-dependent, and completely dependent

Classification Exercise

Directions: Read the paragraph and answer the questions that follow.

Traditional musical instruments can be divided according to how they produce sound into three categories: stringed, wind, and percussion. Stringed instruments produce music through the vibration of taut strings that are plucked, strummed, or bowed. The harp, the guitar, the banjo, and the violin are examples of stringed instruments. The second category contains the wind instruments, which are usually sounded by the player's breath. This category includes the clarinet, the tuba, the trumpet, and so on. The third category—percussion instruments—make sounds when they are struck. Obvious examples of percussion instruments are drums, gongs, and cymbals. Surprisingly, the piano is also considered a percussion instrument because, when the player touches a key, a small hammer inside the piano strikes a string.

1. On what basis does the writer classify musical instruments?

   _____

2. How many categories are there? _____

3. List the categories: _____, _____, _____

4. Which of the following is *not* a transitional expression indicating classification?

   a. obvious examples

   b. the second category

   c. the third category

Answers: Classification Exercise

1. How they produce sound

2. three (3)

3. <u>stringed instruments</u>, <u>wind instruments</u>, <u>percussion instruments</u>

4. obvious examples

Chapter Thirteen

Expository Writing: Argument

Photo by Ekaterina Bolovtsova from Pexels.

What is Argument?

The **argument** or persuasion technique is used to convince an audience to accept a particular point of view or to perform a particular action. An essay that incorporates **argument** takes a **position** on an **issue** and uses valid reasoning that is supported by sufficient evidence.

Key Points for Argument:

- Your ideas or reasons must make logical sense to most readers.
- All of your main points explain your position without getting off track.
- Use facts, quotes, outside research from experts, and illustrative examples to fully explain and support your main points.
- Argument presents your viewpoint or position in one concise sentence called the thesis statement.

More Key Points:

- You must take an identifiable position on your topic and give reasons supported by persuasive information.
- Argument answers the opposition and predicts consequences.
- Clearly and logically support your position with a combination of facts, expert opinions, and examples.

Argument Breakdown Example

Position/Thesis: People should stop smoking, because it is expensive and unhealthy.

Reason #1: Smoking is expensive

- one pack costs over $2
- annually costs $1,000 or more
- accessories cost more money: lighters, ashtrays, matches, etc.

Reason #2: Smoking is unhealthy

- smokers suffer more coughs and colds
- causes cancer, emphysema, and heart disease
- lifespan decreases by seven years

Types of Support for Argument

The argument technique requires sufficient evidence to support your ideas. The amount and quality of the information used determines the efficacy of your argument. Choosing a combination of supportive information from the list below can greatly enhance your powers of persuasion.

Support for Argument:

- **Facts:** Evidence based on objective data regarding a truthful occurrence.
- **Refer to an Authority:** An authority is an expert—an individual or organization—that can be relied on to give unbiased facts and information.
- **Anecdotes or illustrative examples**: Media examples or personal stories should clearly relate to the argument.
- **Predicting the Consequence:** helps the reader visualize the impact or end result that will occur if something does or does not happen.
- **Answering the Opposition:** Anticipate the counter-arguments of critics or opposers to your point of view.

Argument Paragraph Example

The federal minimum wage should be increased to at least $7.50 per hour. First of all, this increase will help families who are living in poverty. Not only will it provide these people with a fairer and more decent rate of pay for their labor, but it will also decrease their need for welfare, food stamps, and other forms of government support. Increasing the minimum wage may also stimulate job growth. According to one 2004 study, states that had boosted their minimum wage above the federal minimum since 1997 actually created 50 percent more jobs than states still at the federal level. That may be because workers who earn more can spend more, which stimulates the economy.

Key Points:

- What is the thesis statement?
- How many reasons support the position?
- What kinds of supportive information are included?

Knowledge Check

Directions: Each of the following sentences tells what you are trying to persuade someone to do. Circle the letter of the reason that seems irrelevant, illogical, or untrue.

1. **If you wanted to convince someone to eat at Lou's Famous Barbeque Restaurant, you could say that...**

    a. the mayor eats at Lou's.
    b. the food at Lou's is very good.
    c. Lou's prices are reasonable.
    d. the service at Lou's is friendly and fast.

2. **If you wanted to convince someone that your town or city is a great place to live, you could say that...**

    a. your town offers many employment opportunities.
    b. you have lived there all of your life, so it's obviously a wonderful place to be.
    c. the crime rate is low.
    d. your town offers many different recreational activities.

3. **If you wanted to convince someone to adopt a dog from the animal shelter, you could say that...**

    a. the adoption fee is reasonable and affordable.
    b. pop singer Kelly Clarkson got her dog from an animal shelter.
    c. by adopting from the shelter, you could save a dog that might otherwise be put to sleep.
    d. the animal shelter offers a wide selection of animals, so chances of finding the right pet are very good.

4. **If you wanted to convince someone that the school day should be lengthened, you could say that...**

    a. doing so would increase student achievement.
    b. extending the school day would save parents money on after-school day-care costs.
    c. a longer school day would solve all of students' problems.
    d. lengthening the school day would help keep older kids out of trouble by reducing the amount of time that they are unsupervised by adults.

Answers: 1. (a)   2. (b)   3. (b)   4. (c)

Argument Exercise

Directions: Read the paragraph and answer the questions that follow.

(1) The Camtrex Corporation should provide day care for the children of its employees. (2) First of all, Camtrex workers need such a program. (3) According to the human resources director, about 850 employees with small children have spouses who also work outside the home; for these workers, day care is a constant problem. (4) Second, the company would undoubtedly benefit from on-site day care since workers could concentrate more fully on their jobs, secure in the knowledge that their children were nearby and well cared for. (5) A program that benefits both employees and management just makes good sense.

1. What sentence states the position? _____

2. How many reasons support the position? _____

3. Give the number of the sentence that is supported by a fact. _____

Directions: Circle the letter of the reason that seems irrelevant, illogical, or untrue.

4. If you wanted to persuade someone to join a particular club on campus, you might say that:

   a. everyone else is joining.

   b. membership would add a valuable extracurricular activity to his or her résumé.

   c. joining would provide opportunities to learn more about a topic of interest.

5. If you wanted to persuade someone to donate money to a certain charity, you might say that:

   a. the charity helps people who truly need it.

   b. the organization manages its money wisely.

   c. the organization's headquarters are in a fashionable part of town.

Answers: Argument Exercise

1. (1)

2. (2)

3. (3)

4. (a)

5. (c)

Chapter Fourteen
Expanding the Details

Photo by Artem Podrez from Pexels.

What are Descriptive Details?

In the previous chapters, we presented several expository techniques to help you move from general, vague prose to more specific and professional writing. Why? Because readers should not be left with questions after reading your document. This is particularly true in the workplace where time is money. Whenever someone stops to ask questions about a memo or an email, they are losing productivity. Basically, bad writing prohibits people from performing their jobs well.

Therefore, clear and specific writing is necessary for everyday interpersonal communication and successful completion of work duties. In the chapter covering the argument technique, you learned what kinds of informative details to include to fully support your position. However, every written document you create must include enough detailed information to clearly convey your purpose for writing. So, if someone asks for more details after reading a document, they are asking for more specific information to help them understand what is being said. Those details take the form of complete sentences that contain enough descriptive words to satisfy a reader's need for complete comprehension.

For example, imagine reading this sentence in a report summary:

"This revision to the child welfare guidelines meets a new requirement by federal law."

What requirement? What federal law? What has been revised?

Notice how this one general, vague statement generates three relevant questions that require a lot more specific detail to properly answer.

How to Give More Details

In college essays, a common request is for students to give more details by adding more support to their paragraphs. Remember, support means more information via complete, descriptive sentences. A well supported paragraph includes quality information that anticipates a reader's questions, meaning the answers have already been provided before anyone can ask. Well-formed paragraphs are the heart of effective writing.

However, a student might feel they have written all they can. *"What more can I write?"* they might ask. *How do I give more details?* Likewise, in workplaces everywhere, team members, administrators, grant writers and co-workers are asking the same questions. In business writing, description goes beyond adjectives or colorful language.

Information that counts as descriptive details include: anecdotes, statistics, quotes, summaries, paraphrases, and facts.

As discussed in previous chapters, the first thing you want to do is answer the six reporter's questions to ensure that you have provided fundamental information to your readers. As a review, here are the reporter's questions.

The Five Ws and One H:
- Who?
- What?
- When?
- Where?
- Why?
- How?

After you have fully examined your document according to the six questions above, you might want to fill in the gaps by providing additional details, depending on the length and complexity of your document. The following section gives examples of the kinds of information that count as description and details.

Kinds of Descriptive Details

Anecdotes: Brief narrative stories from personal experience, history or popular culture found in literature, magazines, books or other printed media. Using extended examples can pique interest in your topic, as well as add additional support to your writing.

Example of Anecdote:

- *Many educational institutions are struggling to make payroll amid reduced state and federal funding. For example, the President of Southern Illinois University encouraged campus officials to curtail non-salary spending to protect the university's ability to meet its payroll (Southern Illinois U. Cuts Spending, 2009).*

Statistics: Bits of information that use numbers to highlight various research studies and reports.

Example of Statistic:

- *According to Smith (2011) in HBCUs Must Embrace Online Education, HBCUs are lagging behind the distance education trend, which compromises their competitiveness against other higher education institutions. Although many HBCU administrators perceive online learning as integral to their long-term goals, only 18 percent of these 105 active institutions offer online courses. In comparison, 66 percent of the nation's two- and four-year postsecondary institutions offer college distance education courses, according to the U.S. Department of Education.*

Quotes: Sentences taken from another author's writing, word for word or verbatim. Journals, magazines, research reports and newspapers are common reference sources for pulling quotes to use in the body of your document.

Example of Quote:

On the other hand, Stuart (2010) contends that many HBCUs are incapable of closing the digital divide. Stuart flatly states, "Closing the so-called digital divide is becoming less of a possibility for many HBCUs." He cites lack of finances as a primary reason for HBCUs lack of adequate technological infrastructure to support online learning or campus wide Wi-Fi.

Summary: A general overview of the main points of a longer piece of writing in your own words. Summaries and paraphrases are often linked together and follow the same principles of not copying someone else's work, word for word.

Original passage:

- Language is the main means of communication between peoples. However, having so many different languages has created barriers to understanding among peoples worldwide. For many years, people have dreamed of setting up an international, universal language which all people could speak and understand. The arguments in favor of a universal language are simple and obvious. If all peoples spoke the same tongue, cultural and economic ties might be much closer, and good will might increase between countries (Kispert, 1990). However, opponents argue that cultural uniqueness will be compromised if everyone is forced to speak one language.

Example of Summary:

- *People communicate mainly through language; however, having so many different languages creates communication barriers. Some think that one universal language could bring countries together culturally and economically and also increase good feelings among them (Kispert, 1990), but at the risk of comprising cultural identity, some argue.*

Paraphrase: In more advanced papers, such as research reports, critical analysis papers or literary critiques, writers must restate outside sources in their own words, without distorting the original meaning of the author's writing. This is called paraphrasing.

Example of Paraphrase:

- *Humans communicate through language. However, because there are so many languages in the world, language is an obstacle rather than an aid to communication. For a long time, people have wished for an international language that speakers all over the world could understand. A universal language would certainly build cultural and economic bonds. It would also create better feelings among countries (Kispert, 1990), but at the risk of sacrificing cultural identity, some argue.*

Facts: Facts are statements that are generally true and can be proven through statistics, research, logic, or scientific inquiry.

Example of Fact:

- There are twelve (12) inches in a foot.

Expanded Paragraph Example

Original: Why I Chose to Attend XYZ College

There are many reasons why I attended XYZ college. The three main reasons are because it's a historical black college which I'm proud to be a part of, they offer all the classes needed for me to reach my degree, and plus I'm from XYZ so I decided to come to this college to reach my goals and be successful. These are all the reasons why I attended XYZ college.

The above paragraph is too short, general and vague.

Better: Why I Chose to Attend XYZ College

It took me a long time to become serious about the need for an education. Supposedly, I am considered a late bloomer. I read in the newspaper and saw on television about what the President was doing at XYZ College. With all the exciting things going on, it seemed to be the place for me. I thought it would be the school that could help me reach my life goals. XYZ College is a progressive institution concerned not only with education of students, but the improvement of life in the community. There has been a tremendous change in the area around the school. There is also a decrease in criminal activity in the neighborhood. Another thing that influenced my decision was the testimonies of current and former students which were all positive. The school size was also influential since I have been out of school for a long time. I considered the teacher/student ratio because I knew I would need a lot of help. Finally, I was influenced by the President's concern for black males. Not many schools care about us unless we are in athletics. I am a parent with children. I need to improve my quality of life so that I can help them. If they see me trying to do well in school, hopefully they will strive to excel also. So far, I think I made a good decision to attend XYZ College.

The above paragraph is much more detailed, descriptive and informative.

Key Points:

- Can you see how the first paragraph is frustrating to read?
- What makes the second paragraph more detailed?
- Do you see how adding details expanded the second example?

Chapter Fifteen
Clear & Concise Writing

Photo by Anete Lusina from Pexels.

What is Clear and Concise Writing?

Clear writing is easy to understand. Concise writing is direct and free of excess wording. Therefore, the goal of clear and concise business writing is to incorporate brevity, description, style, rhythm, and sentence variety to communicate as effectively as possible without overwhelming the reader. Consequently, the techniques presented in this chapter illustrate how to streamline your sentences without sounding dull or robotic by effectively arranging words in a sentence. This arrangement is a matter of style, and effectively stylized sentences improve the overall quality of your writing.

Ultimately, the goal is to produce business writing that is informative and engaging to the reader. Remember, good writing can open doors of opportunity for professional and personal growth, especially in the business world where effective communication is highly regarded. The first two techniques require an understanding of coordination and subordination. Coordination means that two ideas are equally important. Subordination means one idea is more important than the other. To properly demonstrate these relationships within your sentences, you must be familiar with coordinating and subordinating conjunctions, as presented in the chart below.

COORDINATING CONJUNCTIONS	SUBORDINATING CONJUNCTIONS
• for	• after, although, as,
• and	• because, before, if, since
• nor	• then, though, unless
• but	• until, when, whenever, where
• or	• wherever, whether, while
• yet	• who, which
• so	• that

1. Fixing Choppy Sentences

Choppy sentences occur when you write two or more short, simple sentences back-to-back. For the sake of sentence variety and flow, good writing needs a balance of long and short sentences. To increase the readability of your writing, there are **five ways to eliminate choppy sentences**:

- Create two complete sentences.
- Add a comma and coordinating conjunction.
- Add a subordinating conjunction.
- Use a semicolon.
- Use a semicolon and a conjunction.

Key Points:

- If a sentence is too long after combining two shorter ones, you might need to create two separate sentences instead.

- If the ideas are too different to put in one sentence, create two separate sentences that appropriately convey your message.

Choppy Sentence Example:

- Henry and Rose are both in their late thirties. They decided to pay for their own wedding.

Explanation: In the example above, two short sentences can be combined to express one main idea by using one of five grammar and style techniques as illustrated in the chart below.

CHOPPY SENTENCE FIX	SENTENCE REVISION
1. **Create two complete sentences.**	Henry and Rose are both in their late **thirties. They** decided to pay for their own wedding.
2. **Add a comma before a coordinating conjunction.**	Henry and Rose are both in their late **thirties, so** they decided to pay for their own wedding.
3. **Add a subordinating conjunction followed by a comma.**	**Since** Henry and Rose are both in their late **thirties,** they decided to pay for their own wedding.
4. **Use a semicolon to connect two closely related sentences.**	Henry and Rose are both in their late **thirties;** they decided to pay for their own wedding.
5. **Use a semicolon and a conjunctive adverb followed by a comma.**	Henry and Rose are both in their late **thirties; therefore,** they decided to pay for their own wedding.

2. Combining Sentences

Since conjunctions are used to link one sentence part to another, they feature greatly in combining sentences. Depending on the kind of sentence you are writing, coordinating or subordinating conjunctions can reduce wordiness and improve the rhythm of your writing.

Separate:

- The police officers could not explain the cause of the accident. They could not locate a witness.

Combined:

- The police officers could not explain the cause of the **accident, nor** could they locate a witness.

Separate:

- We have rented all the offices. We expect the building to show a profit this year.

Combined:

- **Since we have rented all the offices, we** expect the building to show a profit this year.

Faulty Coordination:

- The team left the huddle, but the school mascot, a goat, ran onto the field.

Correction:

- **As the team left the huddle,** the school mascot, a goat, ran onto the field.

Faulty Subordination:

- Just as the tornado siren blared, Martha put out the cat.

Correction:

- The tornado siren blared **just as** Martha put out the cat.

Faulty Coordination:

- The school board hired a new English teacher **and who** will also coach track.

Correction:

- The school board hired a new English teacher **who** will also coach track.

3. Active/Passive Voice

In **active voice**, the subject of the sentence directly performs the action. The active voice uses the simple or root form of the verb.

Example of Active Voice:

<u>Claire's team</u> <u>cut</u> the budget twenty-five percent.

Who cut the budget? → <u>Claire's team</u> = subject

<u>cut</u> = simple (root) verb

Key Points:

- In **active voice**, the subject of the sentence directly performs the action.

- Active verbs do not include forms of "to be" or helping verbs.

- In **passive voice**, the subject follows the verb and appears to receive the action of the verb. A form of the verb "to be" comes before the main verb.

Example of Passive Voice:

- The budget <u>was cut</u> twenty-five percent by <u>Claire's team</u>.

Example of Active Voice:

- <u>Claire's team</u> <u>cut</u> the budget twenty-five percent.

Active Voice #1:

- Our <u>technical editors</u> frequently <u>update</u> the instruction manuals.

Passive Voice #1:

- The instruction manuals <u>are</u> frequently <u>updated</u> by our <u>technical editors</u>.

Active Voice #2:

- <u>Sherri</u> <u>ate</u> a candy bar.

Passive Voice #2:

- A candy bar <u>was eaten</u> by <u>Sherri</u>.

Active Voice #3:

- The <u>teacher</u> <u>lost</u> my child's final exam.

Passive Voice #3:

- My child's final exam <u>was lost</u> by the <u>teacher</u>.

Key Points:

- In **passive voice**, the subject follows the verb.
- Passive verbs include forms of **"to be."**
- **Forms of "to be"** include the helping verbs *has, have, had, is, be* or *being*.

4. Avoid Vague Language

General language makes the reader feel like something is missing or that more information is needed to make complete sense of your writing. To avoid frustrating your readers in this way, make your writing as specific, exact and vivid as possible. The following tips show you how to enliven your writing with a balanced amount of specific details.

General:

- A <u>car</u> <u>went</u> around the corner.

Specific:

- A <u>battered blue Mustang</u> <u>careened</u> around the corner.

General:

- Janet quickly <u>ate</u> <u>the main course</u>.

Specific:

- Janet <u>devoured</u> <u>a plate of shrimp risotto</u> before her date returned from the restroom.

General:

- <u>She</u> <u>felt good</u> in her <u>new clothes</u>.

Specific:

- <u>Mary</u> <u>felt confident and attractive</u> in her <u>new power suit</u>.

Tips for Avoiding Vague Language

1. Increase your vocabulary.

2. Cross out imprecise or dull words and replace them with more specific terms.

3. Use specific words and phrases.

4. Do not overuse descriptive details.

5. Delete wordy phrases and replace with concise words.

6. Choose the right words.

7. Eliminate clichés.

Add Lively Language

General Verb Example:

- In no particular hurry, Paul and Jane **(walked)** through the botanical gardens.

Lively Verb Example:

- In no particular hurry, Paul and Jane **(strolled)** through the botanical gardens.

General Verbs Example:

- Marva **(is)** at her desk and **(nervously)** watches the clock.

Lively Verbs Example:

- Marva **(fidgets)** at her desk and **(anxiously)** watches the clock.

In the examples below, the underlined word delivers a livelier punch to the sentence.

- The ancient city of Machu Picchu **(<u>perches</u>, hangs, wobbles)** high atop the rugged Andes mountains of Peru.

- The city served not only as a **(hideout, getaway, <u>retreat</u>)** for the nobility, but also as an observatory.

5. Avoid Wordiness

Excessive wordiness refers to unnecessary, repetitious, general words that add nothing to the meaning of a sentence. In contrast, concise writing is specific, exact and descriptive.

WORDY WRITING	CONCISE WRITING
• **Because** of the fact that **the watch was inexpensive** in price, **he bought it.**	• The watch was inexpensive, so he bought it.
• In my opinion, I think that **the financial aid system at Capitol Junior College** is in need of **reform.**	• The financial aid system at Capitol Junior College needs reform.

Delete Clichés

What are clichés? Overused words and phrases that are frequently tossed around in business writing. Another way to avoid wordiness is to eliminate these unnecessary words.

Examples of Clichés

• back to square one	• state of the art
• ballpark	• top dollar
• beyond the shadow of a doubt	• tried and true
• bottom line	• try it on for size
• cost-effective	• under review
• grind to a halt	• vitally important
• richly deserved	• hands-on
• Back to square one	• diamond in the rough

Cliché Revision Example:

• Some people can adjust to the ~~hustle and bustle~~ of city life more than others.

• Extroverted people thrive on the **energy and motion** of city life.

Concise Writing Exercise

Directions: Choose the letter of the sentence that uses the most descriptive language.

1.

   a. Some women cooked food while others took orders.

   b. The older women cooked while the younger women took orders.

   c. The older women fried bacon on the grill, while their granddaughters took orders.

2.

   a. There were crumbs all over the keyboard.

   b. There were cookie crumbs on the computer keyboard.

   c. Cookie crumbs got stuck in the keys of the computer keyboard.

3.

   a. We boarded the shuttle that would take us to Charleston, South Carolina.

   b. We boarded the shuttle, stowed our belongings in the overhead compartment, and prepared for our flight to Charleston, South Carolina.

   c. We got on the plane, stowed our belongings in the overhead compartment, and flew to South Carolina.

4.

   a. Nurses at Beth Israel Hospital met with administrators to request more vacation time.

   b. The nurses asked the hospital administrators for more vacation time.

   c. The nurses asked their bosses for more time off.

5.

   a. We went to the post office, bought stamps, and left.

   b. We walked to the post office, bought two packs of stamps, and went back home.

   c. We went to the post office, bought two packs of stamps, and left.

Answers: Concise Writing Exercise

1. c

2. c

3. c

4. a

5. b

More Resources from
Ashan R. Hampton

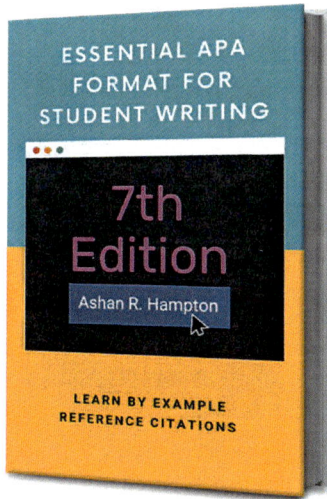

Essential APA Format for Student Writing provides examples of reference citations and samples of student papers. In addition to general APA guidelines, and detailed instruction on in-text citations, grammar and style, this book offers learn-by-example guidance on the fundamentals of APA.

Ordering information:

www.arhampton.com/books

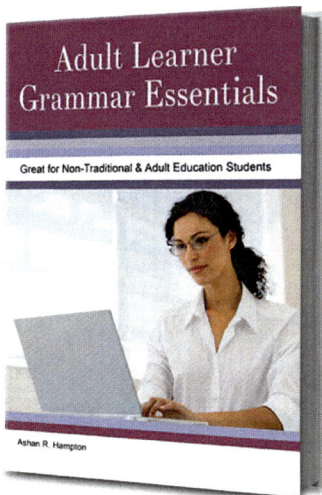

B & W Print, 90 pages
ISBN: 978-1-716-73759-6

Adult Learner Grammar Essentials teaches you to effectively correct the most common grammar errors encountered in academic and professional writing. With self-study quizzes, plain English explanations and real-world examples, you will improve your grammar skills in just minutes a day.

Ordering information:

www.arhampton.com/books

B & W Print, 164 pages
ISBN: 978-0-359-69282-8

References

Collins, T. (2002). *Contemporary's GED Essay: Writing Skills to Pass the Test.* Chicago: McGraw-Hill Contemporary.

Fawcett, S. (2011). *Evergreen: A Guide to Writing with Readings* (9th ed.). Boston: Wadsworth Cengage Learning.

Hampton, A. R. (2018). *Grammar Essentials for Proofreading, Copyediting & Business Writing.* Little Rock: Cornerstone Communications & Publishing.

Research Paper Outline Examples. (2009, January 6). Retrieved from Explorable.com: https://explorable.com/research-paper-outline-examples

Sample of a Paragraph Developed by Definition. (n.d.). Retrieved March 19, 2020, from Athabasca University: http://write-site.athabascau.ca/documentation/Sample%20of%20a%20paragraph%20develope d%20by%20definition.pdf

Thompson Writing Program, Duke University (n.d.) Paragraphing: The MEAL Plan. https://twp.duke.edu/sites/twp.duke.edu/files/file-attachments/meal-plan.original.pdf

Wright, N. (n.d.). *Keep It Jargon-free.* Retrieved Mrch 19, 2020, from Plainlanguage.gov: https://www.plainlanguage.gov/resources/articles/keep-it-jargon-free/

Index

Manufactured by Amazon.ca
Acheson, AB

31070027R00071